The Last Courts of Europe

A Royal Family Album 1860–1914

Introductory text by Robert K. Massie
Picture research and descriptions by Jeffrey Finestone

GREENWICH HOUSE
Distributed by Crown Publishers, Inc.
New York

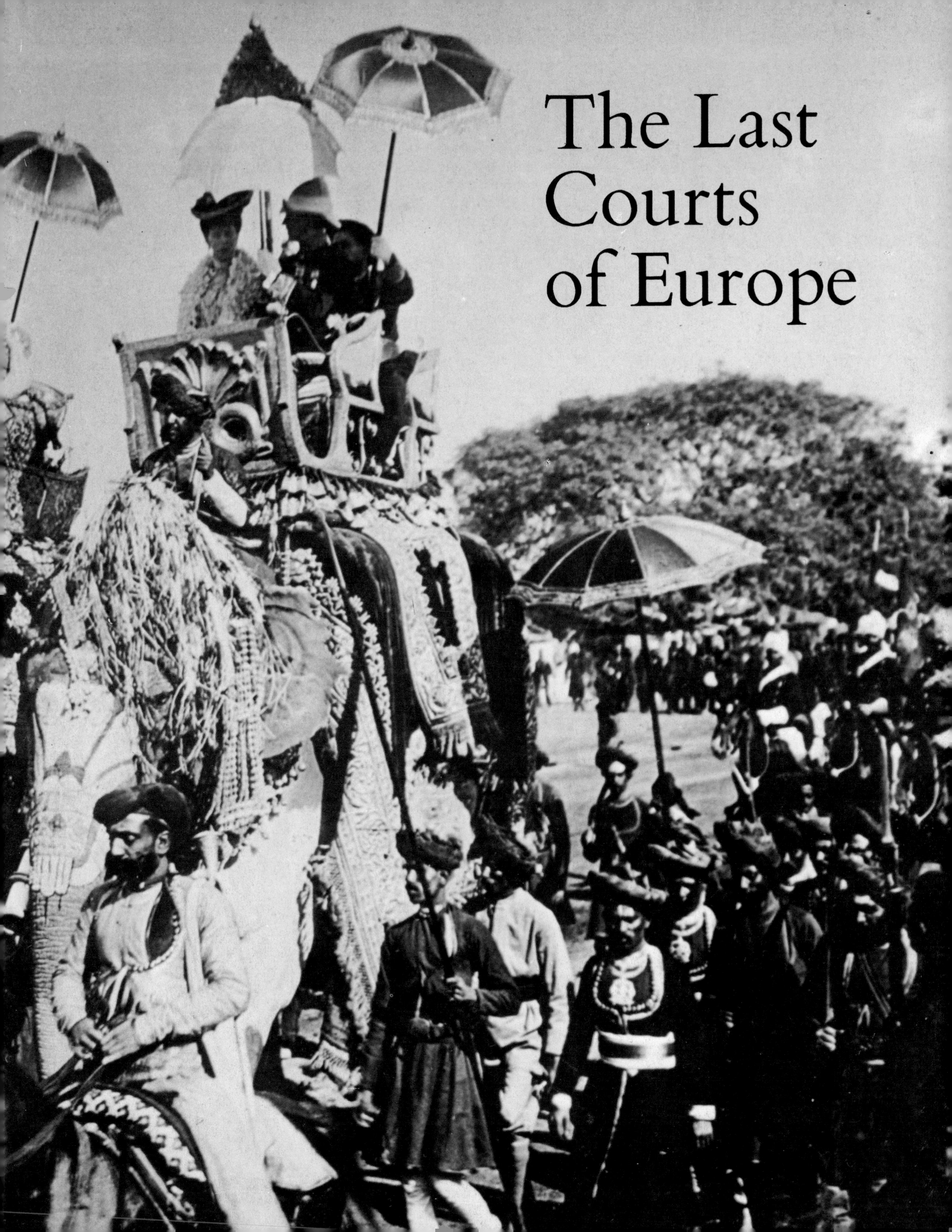

The Last Courts of Europe

First Published in 1981 in Great Britain
by J. M. Dent and Sons Ltd, London

This 1983 edition is published by Greenwich House,
a division of Arlington House, Inc.,
distributed by Crown Publishers, Inc.

Designed and produced by John Calmann and Cooper Ltd.
Edited by Daniel Wheeler and Elisabeth Ingles

Library of Congress Cataloging in Publication Data
The Last courts of Europe.
1. Europe–Kings and rulers–Iconography. 2. Europe–Queens–Iconography. 3. Europe–Princes and princesses–Iconography. I. Massie, Robert K., 1929–
II. Finestone, Jeffrey.
D399.7.L37 1983 940.2′8′0922 83-8983
ISBN 0-517-41472-4

Printed and bound in Italy
by GEA - Milan

Contents

Introduction

Monarchy, these waning years of the twentieth century, counts for little politically. A royal scowl no longer troubles a subject's sleep, nor can a decree from a throne alter the lives of millions. Indeed, there are not many monarchs left. There are no kings or queens at all in North or South America, excepting the curious arrangement by which Canadians swear fealty to the British crown. Three kings (of Morocco, Lesotho and Swaziland) survive in Africa, and only seven monarchs are to be found scattered through the rest of that vast region of palm and pine from the Mediterranean to the Pacific (the Kings of Jordan, Saudi Arabia, Nepal, Bhutan, Malaysia and Thailand, and the Emperor of Japan). All the rest of the world's sceptred monarchs reside in Western Europe, and their kingdoms, ironically, are among the most advanced, industrialized democracies on earth. In this little corner of the planet, the number of crowned heads seems to have stabilized at eight: those of Great Britain, Holland, Belgium, Luxembourg, Norway, Denmark, Sweden, and Spain. In recent years, the total dropped by one when Greece exiled its sovereign and declared itself a republic, but then the number rose again when a new king mounted the throne of Spain.

The population of sitting monarchs may never grow again, but by the same token, it seems unlikely to dwindle rapidly. Those nations which have kept their kings so far, through all the tumultuous upheaval of our century, seem comfortable with the arrangement and likely to retain it for a while. The reason, generally, is that the modern monarch reigns but does not rule. He or she has risen above the abrasive hurly-burly of daily politics and ascended into the shimmering sphere of symbolism and national spirit. 'The King personifies both the past history and the present identity of the Nation as a whole,' proclaims Sir Harold Nicolson. 'The appeal of hereditary monarchy is to stability rather than to change, to continuity rather than to experiment, to custom rather than to novelty, to safety rather than to adventure. The monarch, above all, is neutral.'

It has not always been so. For most of recorded history, kings have been neither few nor neutral. We stumbled out of caves, gathered in tribes, and put ourselves under the rule of monarchs, whether we called them Chiefs, Pharaohs, Moguls, Khans, Sultans, Maharajahs, Caesars, Tsars, Emperors or Kings. Europe conquered the world, planting the flags of its sovereigns in every corner of the globe. The first successful modern revolution against monarchy took place in England's North American colonies, and although the virus would ultimately prove contagious, it was slow to spread. Throughout the nineteenth century, all the European dynasties except the French Bourbons continued to flourish, creating a pageantry and style of life that photography, happily available by mid-century, was able to capture forever.

1 Queen Victoria.

The royal figures portrayed in these pages belonged to an exclusive class of human beings. Most were part of a single, embracing international family (Queen Victoria called it the 'royal mob') in which first cousins routinely married each other, in which kings and emperors were privately known as Bertie, Georgie, Nicky and Willy, and which referred to a little old woman in Windsor Castle as 'Granny'. When the need for a new king arose, as in Greece in 1863 or Bulgaria in 1885, a young male member of an existing dynasty was simply dispatched to mount the throne. In this way, Prince William of Denmark became King George I of Greece, and Prince Alexander of Battenberg became the Prince of Bulgaria. When Prince Alexander did not work out, he was withdrawn and another German Prince, Ferdinand of Coburg, sent to take his place.

In royal marriages, love played a secondary role. It was most agreeable, of course, if a young man and young woman of suitable dynastic credentials could also find themselves in love with each other. But where love failed to develop spontaneously, royal parents and their ministers took the view held by most upper-class parents of the age: suitability counted most; love—or at least an amiable respect—would follow.

Royalty meant hard work. For the major monarchs the routine of public life was ceaseless. Day after day, week after week, month after month, year after year, an endless stream of ceremonies and demands consumed the life of the sovereign, whose every move occurred in the presence of thousands of staring faces and curious eyes, all riveted on each detail of royal behaviour. One escape was into the privacy of palaces, hunting lodges, trains or yachts. Another was the device of *incognito*; that is, taking a false name. This permitted royal persons to travel in foreign countries as ordinary people without the need for ceremonies attendant on state visits. Here they were abetted by an attitude among the press very different from that which prevails today. Regarding Edward VII's private visits to the Continent, one English press lord wrote to the King's private secretary: 'The editors of newspapers are really very glad to receive any hint as to what or what not to publish. Sometimes, when His Majesty is at Marienbad or Biarritz, we shall be very glad to be told what to print and what to omit.'

If the perpetual round of duties or the pressures of office became too great, there was always the possibility of abdication. Queen Victoria, battling her ministers, often threatened to take off her crown and move with her children to Australia. Two emperors, Nicholas II and Wilhelm II, eventually did choose this retreat when the tides of war and revolution swirled around their heads. And assassination was never far from the consciousness of all monarchs. Three American presidents and a Tsar of Russia were murdered within thirty-five years, the Empress of Austria and the heir to the Habsburg throne both fell victim to assassins, a bomb was thrown at Alfonso XIII of Spain and his bride on their wedding day (both were unhurt), and six times during her reign men approached Queen Victoria with intent to do her harm. In Russia the Empress Alexandra never knew, on saying goodbye to her husband in the morning, whether he would return alive that night. Most royal deaths, however, were normal in the sense that kings and queens succumbed to the same illnesses which struck down their subjects: typhoid fever, diphtheria, pneumonia, heart disease, and cancer. Gathered around a deathbed, a royal family felt no concern for titles or rank. The tears that flowed were for mother, father, husband, wife, sister, brother, son or daughter. And that is how these people should be viewed in the words and pictures that follow.

There were four great families in Europe during the twilight years of Western monarchy—Saxe-Coburg-Windsor, Romanov, Habsburg and Hohenzollern—as well as a number of lesser courts spread across the length and breadth of the Continent. My effort in this book has been to recall the lives of the principal figures of the leading dynasties and to re-create the royal world in which they lived. Descriptions of all the courts are provided in brief introductory essays by Jeffrey Finestone, who also sought out the many extraordinary photographs that make up the family album.

The Saxe-Coburg-Windsors

During the latter half of the nineteenth century, the golden afternoon of royal majesty, the monarchs of Europe revolved in stately orbit around the indomitable figure of a woman not five feet tall, Queen Victoria of England. Victoria ruled Europe's most powerful state at the moment of greatest influence in its long national history. Her reign of sixty-four years was a time of unprecedented peace. It was called *Pax Britannica*, but it should have been called *Pax Victoriana*. While she lived, the Queen brought stability and prestige to the crown of England and to all the thrones of Europe. Once she was gone, Armageddon descended and three empires, many kingdoms, and the old system of world order were swept away.

To measure Victoria's achievement properly, one must recall not only what she left at the end of her long reign but also what she had inherited at its beginning. In 1837, when the eighteen-year-old royal heiress mounted the throne, the British monarchy, oldest in Europe, tracing its lineage back to Egbert of Wessex, had teetered and tottered into a state of laughable helplessness. 'From 1812–1837, the Royal Family was held in almost universal contempt,' Professor J. H. Plumb reminds us. The Queen's immediate predecessors on the throne, her grandfather King George III and her uncles King George IV and King William IV, have been ungently but not inaccurately described by Sir Sidney Lee as 'an imbecile, a profligate and a buffoon'.

Victoria's own father, Edward Duke of Kent, fourth son of George III, was no more promising. Retired early from the army because his taste for harsh discipline had caused a mutiny at Gibraltar, permanently in debt, a bachelor at forty-eight, he lived abroad with his mistress of twenty-eight years, a French-Canadian woman named Madame de Saint-Laurent. In 1818, however, inspired by an offer of increased Parliamentary subsidy if he would marry, he ushered Madame de Saint-Laurent to the door and married a thirty-year-old widow, Princess Victoria of Leiningen. Ten months later, on 24 May 1819, a daughter was born. Eight months after that, the Duke of Kent, having made his contribution to the history of England, died of pneumonia.

The little Princess lived with her mother in Kensington Palace, whence she journeyed from time to time to visit King George IV. Early, she knew how to please. Climbing into the lap of the gouty, bewigged old monarch, she would give him a beguiling smile and plant a whispery kiss on his dry, rouged cheek. 'What would you like the band to play next?' the charmed old gentleman once asked. 'Oh, Uncle King, I should like them to play *God Save the King*,' piped the tiny child. 'Tell me what you enjoyed most of your visit,' King George said when it was time for her to go. 'The drive with you,' chimed little Princess Victoria.

She understood that she was different from other children. 'You must not touch these, they are mine,' she announced to a visiting child who was about to play with her toys. 'And I may call you Jane, but you must not call me Victoria,' she added for emphasis. An exasperated music teacher once presumed to lecture: 'There is no royal road to music, Princess. You must practise like everyone else.' Abruptly, Victoria closed the piano lid over the keys. 'There! You see there is no *must* about it!' When she was ten, she discovered and began to study a book of genealogical tables of the Kings and Queens of England. Startled, she turned to her governess and said: 'I am closer to the throne than I thought.' As the governess nodded, Victoria's eyes filled with tears. Then, solemnly, she raised her right forefinger and made the famous declaration: 'I will be good.'

In 1830, when Victoria was eleven, the death of 'Uncle King' brought the Princess even closer to the throne. The new King, her sixty-five-year-old Uncle William, had sired ten children, all illegitimate; Victoria, accordingly, was heir to the crown. William reigned for seven years, but at five in the morning of 20 June 1837, a group of gentlemen arrived at Kensington Palace, having come directly from Windsor where the King had just died. A sleepy young woman in a dressing-gown, her hair still flowing down her back, received them, while they kneeled and kissed her hand. 'I am very young,' the new Queen wrote in her diary that day, 'and perhaps in many, though not in all things, inexperienced, but I am sure that very few have more good will and more real desire to do what is fit and right than I have.'

Young Victoria, brought up without a father, had no qualms about admitting that her good intentions needed the right kind of fatherly guidance. One who gave advice—generally good, always good-humoured—was her dandified Uncle Leopold of Saxe-Coburg, her mother's brother. In 1830, when the people of southern Netherlands had broken away from Holland to create the nation of Belgium, Leopold had been invited to become their King. Victoria's first letter as Queen was to her 'Dearest, Most Beloved Uncle'. King Leopold I wrote back that he would not come to England immediately—'people might fancy I came to enslave you'—but his letters provided a wealth of practical counsel on how to be Queen. A second fatherly figure was Victoria's first Prime Minister, handsome, greying Lord Melbourne. Their relationship was an intoxicating blend of daughter and father, adoring, possessive younger woman and elegant, urbane older man, and—to reverse the drift—sovereign and subject. Melbourne, nearing sixty, had broken many hearts, and his own was deeply scarred. The world took him for a cynic, but he charmed the Queen with his sophistication, his dry wit, and his deep devotion. She proclaimed him 'the best-hearted, kindest and most feeling man in the world', praise endorsed when her beloved spaniel Dash came up to lick Melbourne's hand. 'All dogs like me,' the Prime Minister shrugged, but the Queen would not think it so.

The vicissitudes of politics removed Lord Melbourne, but in 1839 Victoria herself chose the male counsellor who was to have the greatest influence on her life. Her first cousin, young Prince Albert of Saxe-Coburg, had grown up a serious, purposeful child. 'I intend to train myself to be a good and useful man,' he had written in his diary at the age of eleven. Victoria met him when both were seventeen (she was senior by three months, however), and both knew that their elders hoped for a match. Still, the choice was up to her. She felt almost ready to make it when she watched him climbing the stairs at Windsor in October 1839. 'It was with some emotion that I beheld Albert—who is beautiful,' she told her diary. A few days later, the entranced young woman invited Albert to come to her private audience room: 'I said to him that I thought he must be aware *why* I wished them [Albert had come with his brother] to come here—and that it would make me *too happy* if he would consent to what I wished [to marry me].' Albert consented and began the difficult task of being the husband of the Queen of England. He suggested that it would be nice to have a longer honeymoon than the two or three days proposed by the Queen. 'You forget, my dearest Love, that I am the Sovereign and that business can stop and wait for nothing,' reminded Victoria. The couple were married on 10 February 1840, at St James's Chapel, London, and went to Windsor for their wedding night. The following morning the Queen rushed to her diary. Albert had played the piano while she lay on the sofa with a headache, but 'ill or not I NEVER NEVER spent such an evening!!! My DEAREST DEAREST DEAR Albert sat on a footstool by my side, & his excessive love & affection gave me feelings of heavenly love & happiness, I never could have *hoped* to have felt before!—really how can I ever be thankful enough to have such a *Husband*!'

In the early months of marriage, Albert found his position awkward. Victoria adored him and had insisted that the word 'obey' remain in the marriage service, but, as he wrote to a friend, he remained 'the husband, not the master of the house'. Gradually he moved to assert domestic supremacy. His position advanced when, nine months and eleven days after the wedding, Albert became a father as well as a husband. The child was a daughter, Victoria (called Vicky in the family), rather than the hoped-for Prince of Wales, but the defect was remedied eleven and a half months later when Prince Albert Edward, known as Bertie, arrived. The Queen did not enjoy pregnancy and childbirth. 'What you say of the pride of giving life to an immortal soul is very fine, dear, but I own I cannot enter into that,' she grumbled eighteen years later when Vicky wrote rapturously about the birth of her own first child. 'I think much more of our being like a cow or a dog at such moments; when our poor nature becomes so very animal and unecstatic.' Nevertheless, Queen Victoria was often pregnant: six times in her first eight years of marriage; nine times in all. (Vicky and Bertie were followed by Alice in 1843, Alfred in 1844, Helena in 1846, Louise in 1848, Arthur in 1850, Leopold in 1853, and Beatrice in 1857.)

Albert, in addition to counselling his wife in statecraft, took primary charge of training their offspring. His best pupil was his bright, eager, adoring daughter Vicky; his most difficult was the Prince of Wales. The Queen worried that her son 'had been injured by being with the Princess Royal who was very clever and a child far above her age. She puts him down by a word or a look.' Fortunately, Bertie proved to be enormously good-natured, and no permanent rivalry between the siblings resulted. Indeed, brother and sister remained devoted to one another throughout their lives.

The example put before Bertie, in any case, was not his sister but his father. Repeatedly, the Queen urged all her children to emulate this matchless being. 'You may well join us in thanking God for joining to us all your dearest, perfect Father,' she wrote to Bertie when he was fifteen. '*None* of you can *ever* be proud enough of being *the child* of SUCH a Father who has not his *equal* in this world—so great, so good, so faultless. Try, all of you, to follow in his footsteps and don't be discouraged, for to be *really* in everything like him, *none* of you, I am sure, will ever be. Try, therefore, to be like him in *some* points, and you will have *acquired a great deal*.'

Prince Albert, not content simply with serving as an example, devised an inclusive syllabus for his son's upbringing and education, known simply as 'The Plan'. Six days a week were crammed with lessons (Latin, French, German, algebra, geometry, and history, plus the requirement that the pupil write his historical essays in French and German as well as in English).

Meals had fixed hours (9 a.m., 2 p.m., and 7 p.m.) and consisted of specific diets ('meat and vegetables at lunch, a little seltzer water, pudding best avoided'). One memorandum, concerning matters of deportment and dress, declared that 'a gentleman does not indulge in careless self-indulgent lounging ways, such as lolling in armchairs or on sofas, slouching in his gait, or placing himself in unbecoming attitudes with his hands in his pockets.' And every night tutors submitted a written report on the Heir Apparent's work to be inspected by the Queen and her consort.

Bertie struggled to please but often disappointed. When he was seventeen, the Queen wrote to Vicky, who had married Prince Friedrich of Prussia: 'I feel very sad about him. He is so idle and weak.' A year later, she complained, again: 'The greatest improvement, I fear, will never make him fit for his position. His only safety—and the country's—is his implicit reliance in everything on Dearest Papa, that perfection of human beings.' Albert, sending Bertie to visit Vicky, tried to look on the bright side. 'You will find Bertie grown up and improved,' he wrote to his daughter. 'Do not miss any opportunity of urging him to hard work. Our united efforts must be directed to this end. Unfortunately he takes no interest in anything but clothes, and again clothes. Even when out shooting he is more occupied with his trousers than with the game!' During the visit, Prince Albert again described his son to his daughter: 'Bertie has remarkable social talent. He is lively, quick and sharp when his mind is set on anything, which is seldom.... But usually his intellect is of no more use than a pistol packed in the bottom of a trunk if one were attacked in the robber-infested Apennines.'

At nineteen, the Prince of Wales began the first of four terms at Oxford, where his wan effort provoked his father to sigh: 'Bertie's propensity is indescribable laziness. I never in my life met such a thorough and cunning lazybones.' Even Bertie's dutiful submission of his diary for inspection brought Albert's criticism of its lack of critical analysis and reflection. Gamely, Bertie apologized: 'I am very sorry that you were not pleased with my Journal as I took pains with it, but I see the justice of your remarks and will try to profit by them.'

Ironically, Bertie's first independent success came in North America, a substantial segment of which had declared its own independence from his great-grandfather eighty-four years before. In July 1860 the Prince of Wales sailed on a tour of Eastern Canada and the United States. At Niagara Falls he stood on the Canadian side and saw the famous French acrobat Blondin cross from the American side on a tightrope, pushing a man in a wheelbarrow. Blondin proposed that he return with the Prince in his wheelbarrow. Bertie accepted eagerly, but his advisers intervened, and Blondin walked back across the Falls on stilts.

In the United States, then on the verge of civil war, the heir to the British throne travelled incognito as Baron Renfrew, but no one was fooled. In Philadelphia, which he declared to be the handsomest American city he had seen, the audience stood spontaneously and sang 'God Save the Queen'. After passing through Chicago, St Louis, Cincinnati and Pittsburgh, the Prince arrived in Washington where President Buchanan greeted him at the White House and then escorted the royal party to Mount Vernon. In New York, after a parade down Broadway, Bertie was the guest of honour at a ball in the Academy of Music. Two thousand uninvited guests pushed their way in, with the result that just as Bertie arrived, the floor cracked and then sagged three feet. The royal visitor went on to Boston, met Longfellow, Emerson, and Oliver Wendell Holmes, and finally sailed from Portland, Maine, on 20 October. The Queen was proud of her son's success and wrote to Vicky: 'He was immensely popular everywhere and really deserves the highest praise.'

To channel this new nineteen-year-old maturity, the Prince's parents decided that he should be married. Vicky eagerly undertook the assignment of Continental scout, compiling lists of eligible Protestant princesses who might meet her mother's specifications: 'good looks, health, education, character, intellect, and a good disposition'. Eventually, she proposed a candidate: 'She is a good deal taller than I am, has a lovely figure, but very thin, a complexion as beautiful as possible. Very fine, white, regular teeth and very fine large eyes... with extremely prettily marked eyebrows... as simple natural and unaffected as possible ... graceful ... bewitching ... indescribably charming. ...' Queen Victoria, convinced, pronounced the maiden 'a pearl not to be lost'.

The 'pearl' was sixteen-year-old Princess Alexandra of Denmark, eldest daughter of Prince Christian of Schleswig-Holstein. A cousin of King Frederick VII of Denmark, Prince Christian had no money other than the £800 he earned as an officer in the Danish Guards. He lived in an unpretentious house in Copenhagen with a front door opening directly onto the cobbled street. Nevertheless, despite modest circumstances, he managed to bring up six children, four of whom were to sit on thrones: his eldest son Frederick as King Frederick VIII of Denmark, Alexandra as Queen of England, William as King George I of Greece, and Dagmar as the Empress Marie Feodorovna of Russia. During their childhood, Alexandra and Dagmar (called Alix and Minny), three years separate in age, were rarely apart. They shared a small bedroom, made their own clothes together, studied English, German and French side by side, learned music from their mother and gymnastics from their father. Both were trained to love horses. In appearance and character, however, the sisters could hardly have been more different. Princess Dagmar was short, darkly good-looking, clever, and quick-witted, while Princess Alexandra, with her soft brown hair and deep blue eyes, was open, passionately affectionate, sleepily disinterested in books and politics, and, as pronounced by Queen Victoria after seeing a photograph, 'outrageously beautiful'.

Negotiations to acquire the Danish pearl commenced while the husband-to-be was dispatched to spend the summer in training camp with the Grenadier Guards. During this service, a group of sporting young officers spirited a young actress named Nellie Clifden into Bertie's bed. Nellie, who had known a whole regiment of officers, could not help bragging about this particular conquest. In September the Prince departed for Germany and, in company with Vicky, travelled incognito to meet Princess Alix 'by chance' while strolling through a church. Vicky reported the results to Windsor: 'Alix has made an impression on Bertie, though in his own funny and undemonstrative way. He said to me that he had never seen a young lady who pleased him so much.' For the moment that was as far as the Prince was willing to go. Prince Albert wrote sternly to his son, stressing the importance of a marriage and the obvious appeal of this exceptional candidate. Still Bertie held back. The probable cause revealed itself in mid-November when rumours concerning Nellie Clifden, swirling through the clubs of London, reached Prince Albert's ears. He wrote to Bertie 'with a heavy heart on a subject which has caused me the greatest pain I have yet felt in this life.' The malefactor confessed and his father forgave him, encouraging him to 'fight a valiant fight' and go ahead with 'an early marriage. You must not, you dare not, be lost. The consequences for this country and for the world, would be too dreadful!' Albert travelled to Cambridge where Bertie was in residence, took a long walk with his erring son, and came home pleased by Bertie's contrition but physically exhausted. A few days later he wrote to his daughter: 'I am at a very low ebb. Much worry and great sorrow (about which I beg you not to ask questions) have robbed me of sleep during the past fortnight. In this shattered state I had a heavy catarrh and for the past four days am suffering from headache and pains in my limbs which may develop into rheumatism.'

In fact, the Prince had typhoid fever, the deadly killer of the nineteenth century which had afflicted Victoria at the age of sixteen, and which was to strike down so many members of her family. The Queen, in disbelieving horror, sat by his bed while he struggled for breath and called out to her in German. On 14 December 1861 her beloved Albert, only forty-two, died. 'He was my life,' sobbed the Queen. 'How am I alive ... I who prayed daily that we might die together & I never survive him! I who felt when in those blessed Arms clasped and held tight in the sacred Hours at night—when the world seemed only to be ourselves that nothing could part us! I felt so very secure. . . .' Albert's death profoundly changed Queen Victoria's life. 'She called him her father, guide, protector, and even mother,' writes Elizabeth Longford. 'As long as the Prince was alive she did not want to be a mother or even a woman with the full force of her vivid being; only a child, his child.' Now he was gone, and the Queen convinced herself that what she called 'Bertie's fall' was at least in part responsible. 'Oh, that Boy,' she wrote to Vicky, 'much as I pity, I never can or shall look at him without a shudder.'

To remove the offender from his mother's sight, Bertie was packed off for four months to visit Egypt, the Holy Land, and Constantinople. The wedding plans went on, however, and in September 1862 the English Prince met Alexandra in Belgium at the palace of King Leopold. There, walking in the garden, Bertie proposed. He described the moment to his mother: 'After a few commonplace remarks ... I asked how she liked our country, and if she would some day come to England, and how long would she remain. She said she hoped some time. I said that I hoped she would remain always there, and then offered her my hand and my heart. She immediately said Yes. I then kissed her hand and she kissed me.' Two days later, his feelings mounting, Bertie wrote to his mother again: 'I frankly AVOW to you that I did not think it possible to love a person as I do her. She is so good and kind. . . .'

Alexandra arrived in England to become acquainted with the Queen while Bertie was sent off again on another Mediterranean cruise, this time with Vicky and her husband, Prince Friedrich of Prussia. By day the seventeen-year-old Danish girl wrote letters to her fiancé; at night she sat with Victoria and listened to stories about Prince Albert. Her charm captivated the melancholy Queen.

'I can't say how I and we all love her!' Victoria wrote to Vicky. 'She is so good, so simple, unaffected, frank, bright, and cheerful, yet so quiet and gentle that her companionship soothes me. Then how lovely! This jewel! She is one of those sweet creatures who seem to come from the skies to help and bless poor mortals and lighten for a time their path!' To her diary, Queen Victoria gave the ultimate approval: 'How beloved Albert would have loved her!'

When the wedding guests arrived at Windsor, the Queen, feeling 'desolate', did not join them for dinner. But 'dear, gentle Alix knocked at the door, peeped in, and came and knelt before me with that sweet, loving expression which spoke volumes. I was much moved and kissed her again and again.' The day before the wedding Queen Victoria took the engaged couple to the Frogmore Mausoleum where Albert lay enshrined, joined their hands in hers, and declared: '*He* gives you his blessing!' Alexandra considered herself blessed: 'You may think I like marrying Bertie for his position,' she said to Vicky, 'but if he were a cowboy I would love him just the same and marry no one else!'

Marriage and the establishment of a separate household liberated the Prince of Wales from many of the ties that had bound him to his mother. Two homes were created for him: Marlborough House in London and Sandringham in Norfolk, on a 7,000-acre estate purchased for £22,000. While the Queen retired into the shadows of a prolonged grief, society centred itself on the youthful Prince and his beautiful Princess. Bertie, so long repressed, accepted this new role with gusto while Alix, not yet twenty, did her best to keep up. From afar, the Queen clucked disapprovingly: 'Bertie and Alix left Frogmore today, both looking as ill as possible. We are all seriously alarmed about her. For although Bertie says he is anxious to take care of her, he goes on going out every night till she will become a Skeleton .... Oh, how different poor foolish Bertie is to adored Papa, whose gentle, loving, wise motherly care of me, when he was not 21, exceeded everything!'

Ten months after her marriage Princess Alexandra rose abruptly from watching the Prince play ice hockey, rushed home, and was delivered of a seven-month boy, weighing 3 lb 12 oz. In conformity with Queen Victoria's wish that all her male descendants should have the name Albert among their other names, and her female descendants the name Victoria, the child was formally named Albert Victor Christian Edward. In the family, however, he was called Eddy. Unfortunately, the infant's birth coincided with a dramatic political event that deeply—and adversely—affected Princess Alexandra. On 15 November 1863, her father had succeeded to the Danish throne as King Christian IX. Two months later Prussian troops marched into the Danish provinces of Schleswig-Holstein in response to the appeals of the German-speaking Holsteiners for liberation from Danish authority. This little war, which lasted five months and was the first foreign victory for the Prussian Chancellor Otto von Bismarck, painfully divided the British royal family. The Queen and her daughter Vicky, by now Crown Princess of Prussia, were pro-German; Princess Alexandra, weeping bitterly for her own 'poor Papa', swept Bertie, the Government, the press and the British public along on a tide of sympathy for Denmark. Eventually, the Queen enforced domestic peace at Windsor by decreeing that the subject of Schleswig-Holstein be avoided.

Alexandra never forgave the Prussians, and her hatred of the Hohenzollern family burned fiercely all her life. In the summer of 1865, after the birth of her second son, George Frederick Ernest Albert (known as Georgy or Georgie), she travelled with Bertie to Germany. Informed that the Queen of Prussia had come especially to Coblenz to greet them, the Princess of Wales defiantly refused to leave her train. Two years later, again in Germany, she refused to receive a visit from the King of Prussia. This time, the combined weight of her husband and her mother forced Alexandra to give in. Afterwards, looking pale, she was told that she must have caught a cold. 'Yes, I may be pale,' Alexandra replied, 'but it is from anger at being obliged to see the King of Prussia, and not from cold.'

In 1867, near the end of a pregnancy that resulted in the birth of her first daughter, Princess Louise, twenty-two-year-old Alexandra came down with rheumatic fever. The attack began in February, and it was July before she could be wheeled into the garden. Bertie, at first solicitous, soon grew bored. 'The Princess had another bad night,' wrote an indignant lady-in-waiting, '*chiefly* owing to the Prince promising to come in at 1 a.m. and keeping her in a perpetual fret, refusing to take her opiate for fear she should be asleep when he came! And he never came until 3 a.m.!' This prolonged illness left Alexandra with a permanently stiff knee and a limp. Curiously, such was her impact on style that society ladies sought to copy what they called the 'Alexandra limp'. The illness also triggered a form of deafness, hereditary in her family, which grew worse as the years passed, preventing her from full participation in the life of her restless, exuberant husband.

For many years Bertie's life was one of churning, purposeless activity. The Prince of Wales spent an extraordinarily long time—eventually it stretched to fifty-nine years—in the nebulous role of heir to the throne, waiting for an event that he must simultaneously have wished for and dreaded. Meanwhile, the monarchy was split. The tiny, ageing sovereign remained a distant figure, dividing her time between Windsor, Osborne on the Isle of Wight, and Balmoral Castle in the Scottish Highlands. Deprived of Albert, the Queen's character changed. 'When the Prince was alive, she had not been able to choose a bonnet without his advice,' writes Lady Longford. 'Five years later she could not trust her family, her Court, her country, Europe itself to choose a children's nurse, a new fashion or a foreign policy without her advice.' The Prince of Wales was denied any but the most superficial role in government: 'I could hardly bear the thought of anyone helping me or standing where my dearest had always stood,' Victoria later admitted, explaining her treatment of Bertie. Frustrated, the Prince found release for his energy in pleasure and frivolity, shooting, the race-track, yachting, the theatre, card games, and the soft laughter of beautiful women. The Queen complained about the 'Marlborough House fast set', but whenever a Prime Minister attempted to break the pattern by finding real employment for the Prince, his mother balked.

Nevertheless, in her way she loved him. 'Bertie was affectionate and simple and unassuming as ever,' she wrote to Vicky when her son was twenty-eight. 'I am sure no Heir Apparent was ever so nice and unpretending as dear Bertie is.' When he was attacked or when he was ill, Queen Victoria rushed to his side. In October 1871, during his thirtieth year, the Prince came down with typhoid fever. The illness was severe, and on the evening of 11 December the Queen was told that her son probably would be gone before morning. 'In those heartrending moments, I scarcely knew how to pray aright,' she wrote to Vicky, 'only asking God, if possible, to spare my beloved child.'

Barred from serious work, Bertie sought diversion in travel. In 1866 the Prince of Wales journeyed to St Petersburg to represent the Queen at the marriage of Alix's younger sister Minny to the Tsarevich Alexander (known as Sasha) of Russia. Alix, desperately eager to attend, was pregnant and had to remain behind. In 1869, however, she accompanied the Prince on a six-month tour to Paris, Copenhagen, Berlin, Vienna, Cairo, Constantinople, Sebastopol, Yalta, and Athens. In Vienna, Bertie found Habsburg protocol fearsomely rigid—it required him to call upon every member of the Emperor Franz Josef's extended family—and 'as there are 27 archdukes now at Vienna,' he wrote, 'it was hard work.' Alexandra Princess of Wales and Elisabeth Empress of Austria, said to be the two greatest royal beauties, appeared together in public but found little in common except, when visiting the imperial stables, a love of horses. Bertie wrote home to his mother that he had also met the Emperor's heir, ten-year-old Crown Prince Rudolf, 'a very nice young man but not at all good-looking,' who 'was treated almost like a boy by his parents.'

In Egypt six blue and gold river-steamers bore the royal party 500 miles up the Nile, towing barges laden with 3,000 bottles of champagne, 4,000 bottles of claret, four French chefs, four riding horses, and a white donkey for the Princess. Returning to Cairo, Bertie climbed the Great Pyramid, and Alix visited a harem where the ladies painted her face and eyes, wrapped her in a robe and veil, and sent her back to surprise and tantalize her husband.

In 1875 Alix hoped to accompany her husband on his trip to India, but Bertie insisted on exclusively male company. Sartorial elegance was always important to the Prince of Wales, and, admitting that long swallowtail coats would seem odd in the bush, he designed a short dark jacket to be worn with dark trousers and a black bow tie—the birth of the dinner-jacket or tuxedo. In the forests of Nepal, after a day seated in a howdah on the back of an elephant from which perch he shot tigers, the Prince returned to camp, took a hot bath, donned his new dinner-jacket, and presided over a party in his spacious and elegantly furnished tent.

Every year at the end of the London season and after the races at Cowes, Bertie would slip away to a German spa and try to lose weight. He enjoyed meeting his sister Vicky and his brother-in-law Friedrich of Prussia, both of whom he held in great affection, either in Berlin or in some less formal German setting. Aside from Habsburg protocol, he liked the Austrian Emperor. 'The weather is still excellent and the riding enjoyable on manoeuvres,' Franz Josef wrote in 1888 when he was fifty-eight and Bertie forty-seven. 'I tried hard to shake off the Prince of Wales by continued hard trotting and then by sustained gallop. But I didn't succeed. This chubby man kept right up with me. He showed incredible endurance and esprit, even after he grew a bit stiff. He wore through his red Hussar's trousers, which was pretty uncomfortable since he had nothing on underneath.'

Bertie's favourite city was Paris. As a boy of ten, riding in a carriage with the Emperor Napoleon III, he had announced: 'I should like to be your son.' At every opportunity he was off to the French capital, Biarritz and the Côte d'Azur. Wherever he went, unless his visit was a formal, state occasion, the Prince insisted on having personal freedom. This was not a problem in Copenhagen where the entire population behaved like one big family, permitting Bertie and Alix to stroll the streets almost unnoticed. Elsewhere, he used an incognito and became 'Baron Renfrew' or when his wife was along, the 'Duke and Duchess of Lancaster' or even 'Mr and Mrs Williams'.

Even when he became King, Bertie enjoyed ducking out for a free stroll or lunch. In this way he made himself vulnerable to the occasional pitfall, as when, on a visit to Vienna, His Majesty hired a car and made a private visit to a restaurant outside the city. The table had been reserved in the garden under an assumed name, and the restaurant staff did not, in fact, realize the identity of their guest. 'He got very impatient with waiters who merely treated us as ordinary people who had to take their turn,' reported an aide. The lunch became a total fiasco when Edward VII was finally recognized, causing a crowd to gather outside and the village band to strike up 'God Save the King'. As the King gave up and prepared to leave, the whole restaurant rose and cheered.

Travel, however exotic, was not enough to calm the restless Prince of Wales. In the matter of marital fidelity, a curious cyclical pattern manifested itself in the behaviour of the British royal family. Queen Victoria's kingly uncles, monarchs of an older school, surrounded themselves with mistresses and royal bastards. Victoria and Albert, immersed in each other, disdained such practices. Their attempt to give the nation a perfect Prince miscarried, at least on moral matters, and Edward VII enjoyed the favours of many women. His son and successor, George V, was a family man, and it is as wrenching to imagine this sober monarch toying with another woman as it is unthinkable to envision his august consort, Queen Mary, in the arms of a lover. Their son Prince Edward, later King Edward VIII and then Duke of Windsor, achieved a curious sort of compromise, entering into several intense affairs with married women before finally settling down for life with Mrs Simpson.

Bertie's entrapment by feminine allure had come in the person of Nellie Clifden. For several years after his marriage, the Prince found fulfilment in his beautiful wife, but innocent beauty alone could not absorb all of his brimming vitality. Once his wife was hampered by deafness, Bertie grew increasingly bored in her company. She tried to keep up, then fell back, while he went out nightly, stayed late, and was everywhere surrounded by the most ravishing beauties of British society. Temptation often came his way, and often Bertie succumbed.

The rules of British society during the later Victorian era have been admirably explained by Sir Philip Magnus:

> The nineteenth century social code made allowance for frailty in high places by licensing fusion between husband, wife and lover, on condition that no confusion was permitted to occur. Everyone intimately concerned had to be consenting parties, and all who possessed the freedom of Vanity Fair were required to behave with the utmost decorum in order to prevent the innumerable irregular liaisons, which beguiled the tedium of excessive leisure and about which they loved to gossip privately, from becoming publicly known. Any indiscretion which impaired Society's prestige invited a sentence of social death which was ruthlessly executed.

The Prince of Wales's own behaviour faithfully followed these strict rules. His affair with Lillie Langtry, the professional beauty whom he subsequently helped to become an actress, was conducted with the public acquiescence of Edward Langtry, the lady's husband. Nor was there ever any public unpleasantness from the husbands of Lady Brooke (later Lady Warwick) or Mrs George Keppel.

Princess Alexandra also played to perfection her role in these royal bedroom dramas. As long as no public scandal was permitted, she remained gracious and forbearing—even tolerantly amused. An example of her attitude is presented by Georgina Battiscombe:

> One day, she [Alexandra] chanced to look out of the window at Sandringham just as her husband and his mistress were returning from a drive in an open carriage. The Princess herself never lost her graceful slimness but Alice Keppel, her junior by twenty-five years, had already grown very stout, whilst the Prince of Wales had long merited his disrespectful nickname of 'Tum-Tum'. The sight of these two plump persons sitting solemnly side by side was too much for her equanimity; calling her lady-in-waiting to come and view the joke with her, she dissolved into fits of laughter.

It was Alexandra's view that other women did not threaten—indeed, had very little relevance to—her own relationship with 'my Bertie'. On occasion, she could be hurt or exasperated, as when a messy affair developed involving Bertie with Lady Brooke and Lord Charles Beresford, which caused her to prolong a visit with Minny to the Crimea and skip the celebration of her husband's fiftieth birthday. But this was after the scandal had become the talk of London. For the most part, Alix looked the other way or treated the subject lightly, and the nation took its cue from her. Had she displayed resentment against the extramarital adventures, the Prince's public standing could have been severely damaged.

Set partially to one side by her husband, insulated from society by her deafness, the Princess of Wales turned to her children, her horses, and her dogs as the central interests of her life. Before she was twenty-seven, Alexandra had borne six children. The youngest died within twenty-four hours of birth, but on the others—two sons and three daughters—she lavished time and affection.

The two 'Wales boys', as Queen Victoria referred to her grandsons Prince Eddy and Prince George, grew up exceptionally close to each other. Only seventeen months apart in age, they were dressed by the same governess, drilled by the same tutor, and enrolled together as naval cadets. All too soon, however, the difference between them became embarrassingly apparent. Prince Eddy, the heir to the throne, was markedly inferior to his younger brother, not only in academic matters, but in every area of behaviour. Prince Eddy, their tutor Reverend Dalton reported, 'fails, not in one or two subjects, but in all'. A little later Dalton wrote that Prince Eddy 'sits listless and vacant . . . wastes as much time in doing nothing as he ever wasted. . . . This weakness of brain, this feebleness and lack of power to grasp almost anything put before him is manifested . . . also in his hours of recreation and social intercourse. It is a fault of nature.'

Alexandra, often alone, perhaps finding it more difficult to communicate with Eddy, made in her heart a special place for her younger son. It was George who sat with her every morning talking or reading aloud while her long hair was brushed by a maid. They read the Bible together every day, and she went to his room every night to tuck him in bed and hear his prayers. When they were parted, her sadness and his homesickness were revealed in a stream of unusually affectionate and curiously childlike letters back and forth. 'Think sometimes of your poor boy so far away, but always your most devoted and loving little Georgie,' wrote the son. 'What a bad, old Mother dear not to write and you were quite right to say "Naughty, naughty",' replied his mother. When he was eighteen and leaving his mother for a cruise with the Royal Navy, she wrote to him from her bedroom:

My own darling little Georgie:

I have only just left you going to bed after having given you my last kiss and having heard you say your prayers. . . . I need hardly say my darling little Georgie *how* much I shall always miss you—now we have been so much together and you were such a dear little boy not at all spoilt and so nice and affectionate to old Mother dear. Remain just as you are . . . and keep out of temptation as much as you can. . . . And now darling Georgie, I must say Goodnight and Goodbye as I am so sleepy my eyes will hardly keep awake and it is nearly two. So goodbye and God bless you and keep you safe and sound till we meet again and watch over you wherever you are.

Goodbye, goodbye, Georgie dear.

Ever your most loving affectionate old Mother dear.

A naval career had been chosen for this younger son, and he was sent, along with Prince Eddy and a tutor, for three years of cruising to the Mediterranean, the West Indies, South America, Australia, Japan and China. He lived with his brother in a small cabin under the poop, slept in a hammock, dined in the midshipmen's mess on the traditional salt pork and biscuits, did rifle and cutlass drill, and helped shift topsails in the face of a storm. In Barbados the two Princes visited the local botanical garden and sniffed a large, heavily pollinated lily. A journalist observed them, their noses covered with yellow pollen, and telegraphed to England that the royal boys had been tattooed. The Queen and the Prince of Wales were furious, but Princess Alexandra responded lightly: 'How could you have your impudent nose tattooed,' she wrote to Georgie. 'What an object you must look and won't everybody stare at the ridiculous boy with an anchor on his nose! Why on earth not have put it somewhere else?' Two years later, in Jerusalem, the tattoos became real. 'We have been tattooed,' wrote George to his mother, 'by the same old man that tattooed Papa and the same thing too, the five crosses. You ask Papa to show his arm.'

At home, Queen Victoria's long reign stretched on and on, and Bertie, an intelligent, curious, enormously energetic man now in his fifties, still had nothing serious to do. 'The Prince of Wales writes to me that there is not much use his remaining at Cowes (though he is willing to do so) as he is not of the slightest use to the Queen,' wrote one of his aides to another in 1892. 'Everything he says or suggests is pooh-poohed.' There were those—Mr Gladstone, the Prime Minister, among them—who believed privately that the Queen should abdicate, but despite her threats when crossed to do so, Victoria had no such intention. Indeed, her majesty continued to wax: she became Empress of India in 1877; her Golden Jubilee was celebrated in 1887; and her Diamond Jubilee (sixty years on the throne) in 1897. She went on to the age of eighty-one, outliving three of her nine children. (Alice, who married the Grand Duke of Hesse, died of diphtheria in 1878; Leopold, Duke of Albany, died in 1884 of complications caused by his haemophilia; Alfred, Duke of Edinburgh, died of cancer of the throat in 1900.) The great Queen's own death finally came on 22 January 1901, her family assembled around her bed, the Prince of Wales kneeling at her side, the German Emperor, her grandson, supporting her with a pillow in his arms. 'The last moments,' an observer reported, 'were like a great three-decker ship sinking. She kept on rallying and then sinking,' recognizing people, calling their names, then gasping for breath and closing her eyes. When she was gone, the Kaiser and the new King Edward VII themselves lifted her into her coffin.

The coronation of Edward VII was postponed by his own illness. A chronic sufferer from bronchitis and overweight, he seemed unable to cut back. He had always been a *gourmand*, consuming twelve courses at dinner and taking special delight in caviar, truffles, foie gras, grilled oysters, and rich sauces. During a normal day, His Majesty smoked twenty cigarettes and twelve gigantic cigars. His chest and stomach were of equal girth: 48 inches. Twelve days before the ceremony in Westminster Abbey, he caught a chill and lost his appetite. His doctor diagnosed appendicitis, but the King would not hear of any operation which would postpone the coronation. Finally, three days before the date, informed that he would die without immediate surgery, the King consented, and in three-quarters of an hour, the job was done. By the next afternoon, 'I found him smoking a cigar and reading the paper,' reported Prince George. Two months later the King was crowned. As he dressed himself in his robes, sashes, sword and medals before starting for the Abbey, his grandchildren were sent in to see him. 'Good morning, children,' he said, 'Am I not a funny-looking old man?'

As King, Bertie adopted a routine that took on a regular annual pattern. The winter months were spent at Sandringham, Windsor, and Buckingham Palace. In March he left for Paris, Biarritz, and a month's cruise on his yacht in the Mediterranean. In May he returned to London for the Season, attending Ascot in the middle of June and in August presiding over the annual regatta at Cowes. Late in August and early in September, while Queen Alexandra joined her sister Minny in Denmark, the King dieted at a German spa. He hunted grouse and deer at Balmoral in October, then for the holidays went to Sandringham and London. He travelled in a string of three comfortable private coaches accoutred with thick carpets, deep leather chairs, bathrooms, a bar, and many cases of cigars. In his claret-coloured cars he enjoyed taking fast drives with his chauffeur-engineer, Stamper. 'A very good r-run, Stamper. A very good r-run indeed,' the King would say on returning from a spin.

It was easy for those around the King to learn his mood. A gay, infectious laugh and a nodding 'Yes, yes, yes!' proclaimed his pleasure, while boredom was expressed by a rapid drumming on the table with his plump fingers. Consuelo, the young American Duchess of Marlborough, recalled his visits to Blenheim Palace: 'I had the . . . [King] as my neighbour for each meal. It must have been trying for him day after day. He was interested in gossip and politics—and liked to hear the latest scandal, which at nineteen I was unlikely to know. He had a disturbing habit—drumming hard on the table with his fingers—and if I thought of something to say and turned to him, he would say, "Yes, my dear lady; yes, my dear lady," staring down the length of the table.'

2 King Edward VII.

3 Queen Alexandra.

The one person whom Edward VII could neither dominate nor intimidate was his wife. To the King a rigidly planned, precisely executed schedule was the cornerstone of daily life. Queen Alexandra was vague, impulsive, unmethodical, and decidedly unpunctual. And although she knew that these habits exasperated her husband, she made no attempt to change them. 'Keep him waiting, it will do him good,' she once declared to a courtier who reminded her that His Majesty had been waiting for half an hour. Always twenty or thirty minutes late for dinner, she could be even more dilatory on formal occasions. Sir Frederick Ponsonby describes a scene at the palace where the King and Queen were to receive a number of deputations:

> The King came down in full uniform . . . but when it came to twelve o'clock there was no sign of the Queen. Meanwhile the second deputation arrived and then the third, fourth, and fifth . . . and soon every room was filled with eminent men in uniform, but in spite of repeated messages there was no sign of the Queen. The King in full uniform sat in the Equerries' room drumming on the table and looking out of the window with the face of a Christian martyr. Finally at ten minutes to one, the Queen came down looking lovely and unconcerned. All she said was, 'Am I late?' The King swallowed and walked gravely out of the room.

Now that she was Queen, Alexandra was more often able to visit the person, other than her children, to whom she felt closest, her sister Minny. In 1873 Minny had gone to London with her husband, the Tsarevich Alexander, and the two sisters delighted society by dressing identically, both day and evening. In 1874 Alix and Bertie returned the visit, in the course of which the Princess of Wales wrote delightedly to Prince Eddy about the famous Russian ice mountains in St Petersburg: 'Aunt Minny and [I] drive in sledges every day and skate too, and then we are driven down some steep icebergs on little chairs which is most amusing.' Copenhagen was a regular summer meeting-place for the sisters and their families. Alexandra wrote to Prince George in 1883 of 'that *awful* moment of tearing ourselves away from one another, not knowing *where* and *how* our next meeting may be. Poor little Minny, I can see her now, standing on the top of the steps in utter despair, her eyes streaming with tears, and trying to hold me as long as she could.' Alexandra was in the Crimea in 1894 when Sasha's death left Minny a widow at forty-four, and helped to nurse her through the first months back in St Petersburg. In 1907 Minny, as Dowager Empress, came to visit England and wrote home to her son, Nicholas II: 'How happily we are all living together! I have no words to describe how magnificent it all is [at Windsor]. Aunt Alix's rooms are remarkably beautiful and cosy—I must say they are the same here, at Buckingham Palace. Everything is so tastefully and artistically arranged—it makes one's mouth water to see all this magnificence.' That same year, their father, eighty-eight-year-old King Christian IX, finally died, and their brother moved into the Amalienborg Palace as King Frederick VIII. In order to have a home of their own in Denmark, the two sisters bought a holiday villa, Hvidore, outside Copenhagen. It was to this place that Minny retreated after war and revolution had destroyed her life in Russia.

The years went by, but Queen Alexandra never got over her hatred of Prussia. When the Kaiser made her son Prince George an honorary Colonel in a Prussian regiment, Alexandra sputtered: 'And so my Georgie boy has become a real life, filthy, blue-coated, Pickelhaube German soldier!!! Well, I never thought to have lived to see *that*! But never mind, as you say it could not have been helped—it was your misfortune and not your fault.' When Kaiser Wilhelm II came to Sandringham she was maliciously gleeful to discover that he was bringing with him a second hairdresser to wax and bend his distinctive moustache. 'Ach, the fool!' she laughed. Once when Wilhelm was speaking to her long and earnestly, she waited until he finished and then smiled at him: 'Willy dear, you know that you always speak rather indistinctly. I am afraid I have not heard a single word you were saying.'

To the end of her life Queen Alexandra retained her uninhibited, warm-hearted nature. As Princess of Wales, she visited John Merrick, the unfortunate 'Elephant Man', became his friend, and wrote him a card every year at Christmas. Visiting a hospital during World War I, she approached a patient depressed because a wound in his knee had made his leg permanently stiff. 'My dear, dear man,' said Her Majesty, 'I hear you have a stiff leg; so have I. Now just watch what I can do with it.' So saying, she hoisted her skirt and swung her own stiff leg in a dazzling arc over the top of his bedside table.

Alexandra's sympathetic spirit was never better exhibited than at the moment of Bertie's death. The King had been stricken with severe bronchitis followed by a series of heart attacks. After his doctors abandoned hope, he sat hunched in an armchair through a long afternoon, while his family and friends came to say goodbye. Before his consciousness faded, Queen Alexandra—in one of the most generous gestures ever made by any wife—sent for Mrs Keppel so that she too could bid farewell.

The succession to King Edward's throne was provided, many thought, by Special Providence. In the normal sequence, Prince Eddy, despite his defects of intelligence and character, would have worn the crown. Assuming this to be the case, his family were keenly interested in whom he would choose to be his bride. At first, Eddy had been attracted to his golden-haired cousin, Princess Alix of Hesse, but she firmly rejected his suit. Next, Eddy fell in love with Princess Hélène, daughter of the Comte de Paris, pretender to the throne of France. Although Hélène was a Roman Catholic, she promised to convert to the Church of England. Princess Alexandra was enthusiastic, the Prince of Wales approving, and Queen Victoria consented. Unfortunately, the Comte de Paris did not like the idea of her conversion, and when the Pope flatly refused, the affair was dropped.

Queen Victoria then took charge of the matter, looked over the list of eligible Protestant royalty, and chose tall, quiet, serious Princess Mary (called May) of Teck as best qualified. '[She is] far preferable to *ein kleines deutsches Prinzesschen* with no knowledge of anything beyond small German courts,' declared the Queen. Prince Eddy, then twenty-seven, proposed and became engaged in November 1891.

That same month, Prince George was stricken by typhoid

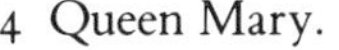

4 Queen Mary.

5 King George V.

fever. Princess Alexandra, visiting Empress Marie in the Crimea, rushed home. After a week of uncertainty, the young man rallied. Then in January at Sandringham, Prince Eddy came down with influenza. Four days later it was pneumonia, and on 14 January 1892, Queen Victoria received a telegram at Windsor from the Prince of Wales: 'Our darling Eddy has been taken from us.'

George and May had stood by Eddy's deathbed, and the younger brother was stunned by what had happened. 'No two brothers could have loved each other more than we did,' he wrote to Queen Victoria. 'I remember with pain every hard word & little quarrel I ever had with him & how I long to ask his forgiveness, but, alas, it is too late now.' Not only did he have to cope with his great loss, but he had suddenly inherited all of Eddy's future: he, who had served fifteen years in the Royal Navy without ever imagining he would rule anything larger than a quarterdeck, was now heir to the throne after his father. As such, it was now *his* duty at twenty-six to marry and provide the monarchy with continuity and a future. Here Queen Victoria did not hesitate. She had chosen May of Teck for Eddy; she would do equally well for George. Fifteen months after Eddy's death, on 6 July 1893, George and May were married. On 23 June 1894, Prince Edward Albert (known in the family as David) was born.

Queen Victoria and Princess Alexandra each treated the marriage according to character. The aged Queen, thinking practically, wrote in May 1894 to Vicky: 'She [May] strikes me more and more as very clever & so sensible & right-minded & is a great help to Georgie, helping him in his speeches and what he has to write.' Alexandra, generously giving up one son to another woman soon after having lost her first, wrote: 'I pray to God to give you both a long and happy life together and that you will make up to dear May all that she lost in darling Eddy.'

This was a heavy burden of responsibility to impose upon the grieving Prince, but he told his parents that he felt he could love someone who would be able to love him. He soon found himself succeeding. 'I adore you, sweet May,' he wrote to his wife in the first years of marriage. 'Georgie is a dear,' the cool, even-tempered May wrote to her old governess. 'He adores me which is quite touching.' In 1911, after eighteen years of marriage, King George congratulated Queen Mary on the success of their partnership: 'We suit each other admirably & I thank God every day that He should have brought us together, especially under the tragic circumstances of dear Eddy's death & people only said I married you out of pity & sympathy. That shows how little the world really knows what it is talking about.'

The Hohenzollerns

'Oh, Madam, it is a Princess,' announced the physician who presided over the delivery of Queen Victoria's first child.

'Never mind,' came the crisp reply of the twenty-one-year-old Queen, still energetic after twelve hours of labour. 'The next will be a Prince.'

The Queen was not to be denied and Bertie appeared less than twelve months later. But her favourite child, and that of 'Dearest Albert', was the first little girl, Victoria Adelaide Mary Louise, who was known as Vicky and who grew up to become Empress of Germany.

Vicky especially belonged to Albert. He was enchanted with this bright little girl who was able to speak three languages at the age of eight. Not only was she the most intellectual of his children, the pupil and companion with whom he could discuss politics, art, music, science and religion, she was also to become the instrument of his Grand Design. Albert dreamed of a Europe united in liberalism, progress and peace. The constitutional monarchy of a liberal England would become one of the twin pillars of this noble edifice; a united Germany, gathered under the leadership of a newly liberalized Prussia, would be the other. The King of Prussia, Friedrich Wilhelm IV, and his brother, who would take the throne as the Emperor Wilhelm I, were both rigidly conservative, but were growing old. The future lay with Wilhelm's son, young Prince Friedrich. And Friedrich, if not dazzlingly intelligent, was handsome, amiable, and dutiful—a man, Albert felt sure, who could be steered by the right clear-headed, purposeful wife: someone like Vicky.

Fritz, as Prince Friedrich was known, met Vicky at the Great Exhibition in 1851 when he was twenty and she only ten. Four years later, walking through the heather on a hillside near Balmoral, the blond Prussian Prince proposed to the fourteen-year-old Princess Royal. The wedding, delayed until the bride had reached seventeen, took place on 25 January 1858 in St James's Chapel. At the end of the ceremony the newly-weds left the church to the strains of Mendelssohn's 'Wedding March', the first time the music composed for Shakespeare's *A Midsummer Night's Dream* had been used for this serious purpose. Vicky departed for Germany on a river of tears. The Queen wept as she embraced her daughter; the bride wailed, 'I think it will kill me to take leave of dear Papa'; and Bertie sobbed as he stood beside his father on a Channel quay, waving at the boat which was carrying his sister across to the Continent. Only Albert remained in control, but then he dashed back to Windsor to write to his beloved daughter: 'I am not of a demonstrative nature and therefore you can hardly know how dear you have always been to me.'

Vicky's reception in Prussia was cool. *Junker* pride had been offended by Queen Victoria's insistence that the wedding of a future Prussian Crown Prince take place in London rather than Berlin. Despite the long engagement, no home had been prepared, and the young couple spent their first winter in a dark, cold, ancient castle. 'The rooms were immense, the walls covered with full-length pictures, the great furniture creaked, and the wind on a winter's night shrilled through the ill-fitting doors and windows,' wrote a lady-in-waiting who suffered with them.

On 27 January 1859, Vicky—now eighteen—gave birth to a son, an infant who was to become the extraordinary individual we know as 'the Kaiser'. A long and difficult labour had been endured without anaesthetics (Prince Friedrich held his suffering wife in his arms through many of those hours), when finally the doctors decided to use forceps. In the end, the child was extracted, but he arrived with severe damage to his left arm: the tiny limb had been wrenched almost out of its socket.

This was the first grandchild of the Queen of England (who was still only thirty-eight), and, according to her wish, the baby bore the name of Albert. Christened Friedrich Wilhelm Victor Albert, he was known in the family as Wilhelm, but the Queen was satisfied. She first saw him at twenty months. 'Our darling grandchild . . . came walking in . . . in a little white dress with black bows. . . . He is a fine fat child with a beautiful white, soft skin, very fine shoulders and limbs, and a very dear face, like Vicky and Fritz. . . . he has Fritz's eyes and Vicky's mouth and very fair, curly hair.' When Wilhelm was two and a half, Vicky brought him to Osborne, where Grandfather Albert wrapped him in a large white damask table-napkin and swung him back and forth as the little boy screamed with pleasure and his grandmother clucked her smiling disapproval.

At four, Wilhelm was brought back to England to be present at the wedding of his Uncle Bertie to Princess Alexandra, for whom his own mother had played matchmaker. Wilhelm attended the ceremony wearing a Highland costume, a gift from his grandmother, which included a small toy dirk. During the ceremony, Wilhelm was restless. His eighteen-year-old Uncle Alfred, Duke of Edinburgh, appointed to keep an eye on him, told him to be quiet, but Wilhelm drew his dirk and threatened his guardian. When Alfred attempted to subdue the rebel by force, Wilhelm bit him in the leg. The Queen missed seeing this little fracas, and to her Wilhelm remained 'a clever, dear, good little child, the great favourite of my beloved Angel [Vicky].'

Vicky steadily produced a squad of siblings for her son to play with. Wilhelm was followed by Charlotte in 1860, Henry in 1862, Sigismund in 1864, Victoria in 1866, Sophie in 1870, and Margaret in 1872. In a sense, Vicky also mothered Fritz, who loved and admired his scintillating wife, treated her as an equal in public, and deferred to her in private. She herself was happy. 'Not a hope has been disappointed. Not an expectation that has not been realized,' wrote Albert's favourite child on the third anniversary of her wedding.

By then, however, Vicky's world had changed. In January 1861 Friedrich Wilhelm IV had died, which brought his sixty-year-old brother to the throne as King Wilhelm I. Fritz, at thirty, and Vicky, at twenty, now became Crown Prince and Crown Princess of Prussia, expecting within a few years to mount the throne themselves and fulfil Prince Albert's Grand Design. But the elderly King ruled on and on—for twenty-seven years—and he delegated the real power of the state to his Chancellor, Otto von Bismarck. Bismarck united Germany, as Albert had dreamed, and in 1871 made his master Emperor, but it was a rigidly conservative rather than a liberal political union that the Iron Chancellor created. Vicky vigorously opposed Bismarck's policies, the more so because in February 1861, her own 'Dearest Papa' had been snatched away. Grief gave her father's lessons the force of A Voice from Heaven and the young Englishwoman set herself compulsively to obstruct and reverse the course of Prussian and German affairs. Nevertheless, she strongly supported Bismarck's wars against Denmark, Austria and France, and when Fritz became a hero at the Battle of Sadowa, Vicky burbled delightedly: 'I feel that I am now every bit as proud of being a Prussian as I am of being an Englishwoman and that is saying a very great deal as you know what a "John Bull" I am. . . . I must say the Prussians are a superior race as regards intelligence and humanity, education and kind-heartedness.'

When Wilhelm was eight, Vicky allowed herself some pride: 'Willy is a dear, interesting, charming boy—clever, amusing, engaging—it is impossible not to spoil him a little.' She worried dreadfully about his arm, which, despite painful electric-shock treatments, failed to grow and remained limp. 'I am sure you would be pleased with William if you were to see him,' she wrote to her mother when the boy was twelve. 'He has Bertie's pleasant, amiable ways—and can be very winning. He is not possessed of brilliant abilities, nor any strength of character or talents, but he is a dear boy and I hope and trust will grow up as a useful man. . . . He has very strong health and would be a very pretty boy were it not for the wretched, unhappy arm which shows more and more, spoils his face . . . his carriage, walk and figure, makes him awkward in all his movements, and gives him a feeling of shyness, as he feels his complete dependence, not being able to do a single thing for himself. It is a great additional difficulty in his education, and is not without its effect on his character. To me it remains an inexpressible source of sorrow!'

Despite his useless arm, Wilhelm steeled himself to learn to ride, shoot, swim and fence. With his brother Henry, he embarked on a rigid course of schooling: twelve hours a day beginning at six in the morning. His English was that of an Englishman, and he often read to his mother from Tennyson, Walter Scott or Macaulay, as she painted at her easel. His manners were good—'It is impossible to find two nicer boys than William and Henry,' declared the Prince of Wales—and his morals pure. He disapproved of the promiscuous life of his friend Crown Prince Rudolf of Austria. 'I am forced to notice . . . that he did not take religion seriously. . . . Nor could I help becoming aware of other faults of character so much as to destroy my original confidence, and we drifted further and further apart.' He disliked Paris: 'The feverish haste and restlessness of Parisian life repelled me.'

When he was nineteen and a student at Bonn University, Wilhelm fell in love with his cousin, Princess Elisabeth of Hesse. Ella, as she was called, found him impossibly overbearing. He would ask to ride, then demand to shoot, or row or play tennis. When he was bored, he would climb off his horse, or throw down his racquet and announce that everyone should sit about him while he read aloud from the Bible. Whatever he was doing, he always wanted his cousin Ella next to him. His suit made no progress and years later, when he was Kaiser and she the wife of Grand Duke Sergei of Russia, he stubbornly refused to see her. As an old man, Wilhelm admitted that he had spent much of his time in Bonn writing love poetry to his beautiful cousin.

Rejected by Ella, Willy immediately turned elsewhere. Within four months of leaving Bonn, he was engaged to Princess Auguste Viktoria of Schleswig-Holstein, a simple, rosy-cheeked girl known as Dona, who was to love her husband unquestioningly and devote her life to her clothes and her children. 'She is just like a good, quiet, soft cow that has calves and eats grass slowly and ruminates,' declared an Englishwoman who had married a German prince. 'I looked right into her eyes to see if I could see anything behind them, even pleasure or sadness, but they might have been glass.' There was no passion on Wilhelm's part, but he was fond of Dona and compared her submissive attitude favourably with his mother's treatment of his father.

Increasingly, Vicky and her eldest child began to clash. 'My mother and I have the same characters,' Wilhelm later explained to the British Ambassador. 'I have inherited hers. That good, stubborn English blood which will not give way runs in both our veins. The consequence is that if we do not happen to agree, the situation becomes difficult.' Although he was now a man, Vicky continued to lecture to and patronize her son. 'William is as blind and green, wrong-headed and violent on politics as can be,' the Crown Princess wrote to her mother, using language which must also have fallen on Wilhelm's ears. Bismarck sensed the tension and played up to Wilhelm, inviting him to breakfast, then reclining on his couch and permitting the young Prince to light his pipe for him. Cleverly, the Chancellor used Vicky's constant complaints about Germany and German character to create an image of a highly placed Englishwoman deliberately using her position and her husband to manipulate German policy for the benefit of England. Even Fritz's private secretary scorned his master's submissiveness to his wife. 'You only have to look at what she's made of him,' he declared. 'But for her, he'd be the average man, very arrogant, good-tempered, of mediocre gifts and with a good deal of common sense. But now he's not a man at all, he has no ideas of his own, unless she allows him. He's a mere cipher.'

Early in 1887 Fritz had trouble speaking and clearing his throat. His doctors found a small growth in the larynx and burned it off with a hot wire. When the Crown Prince's hoarseness persisted, they proposed to go ahead and remove the larynx, an operation which would have left the patient permanently voiceless. An English specialist was called in and, to Vicky's joy, declared the growth not cancerous and surgery unnecessary. Permitted to attend Queen Victoria's Golden Jubilee, Fritz rode through the streets of London in an eagle-crested helmet and a white uniform with silver breastplate, reminding the English crowd of Charlemagne or Lohengrin. He remained two months in England and then went with Vicky to a villa in San Remo to spend the winter in the Italian sun. There, the trouble reappeared, and seven doctors and fifty journalists soon arrived. The same English doctor was summoned; this time, however, he admitted that the patient unquestionably had cancer. Alone together after receiving the news, Fritz and Vicky wept and clung to each other. 'To think that I have such a horrid, disgusting illness! That I shall be an object of disgust to everyone and a burden to you all! I had so hoped to be of use to my country,' Fritz shuddered. To her mother Vicky wrote: 'My darling has got such a fate before him which I hardly dare to think of.'

The diagnosis had just been announced when Wilhelm suddenly arrived at San Remo. Throughout his father's illness, he had been upset that his mother had chosen to follow the advice of an English rather than a German doctor. Now, hearing the diagnosis, he tried to rush to his father's side: 'My arrival gave little pleasure to my mother.... Standing at the foot of the stairs, I had to allow the flood of her reproaches to pass over me, and to hear her decided refusal to allow me to see my father.... Then I heard a rustling at the top of the stairs. I looked up and saw my father smiling a welcome to me. I rushed up the stairs and with infinite emotion we held each other and embraced.'

Vicky described the same scene to her mother: 'You ask how Willy was when he was here. He was as rude, disagreeable and as impertinent to me as possible when he arrived, but I pitched into him with, I am afraid, considerable violence and he became quite nice and amiable and gentle (for him).... He began with saying ... [that] he had to speak to the doctors. I said the doctors had to report to me and not to him, upon which he said that he had the "Emperor's orders" ... to report ... about his Papa. I said it was not necessary, as we always reported to the Emperor ourselves. ... I said I would go and tell his father how he behaved and ask that he should be forbidden the house—and walked away.'

'... W. is of course much too young and inexperienced to understand all this. He was merely put up to it at Berlin. He thought he was to save his Papa from my mismanagement. When he has not his head stuffed with rubbish from Berlin, he is quite nice and *traitable* and then we are pleased to have him; but I will not have him dictate to me—the head on my shoulders is every bit as good as his.'

Seven months later the 'young and inexperienced' Willy was Emperor of Germany. Events moved quickly. In February 1888 an operation was performed on Fritz which cost him his voice, but prolonged his life by permitting him to breathe through a tube inserted into his throat. In March the nonagenarian Emperor Wilhelm I finally died and Fritz, now fifty-seven, became the Emperor Friedrich III. Queen Victoria was ecstatic that, after so long a wait, her daughter's patience had been rewarded: 'My own dear *Empress Victoria* it does seem an impossible dream, may God bless her! You know *how* little I care for rank or Titles but I cannot *deny* that *after all* that has been done and said, I am *thankful* and *proud* that dear Fritz and you should have come to the Throne.' The new Emperor and Empress returned to Berlin, but those who saw their tall sovereign knew that his days were numbered. On 24 May Friedrich attended the wedding of his son Henry to Princess Irene of Hesse wearing a uniform whose collar was cut high enough to cover the tube in his throat, but his emaciation and feebleness were evident. On 15 June 1888, after a reign of only ninety-nine days, Friedrich III died and was succeeded by his son, Wilhelm II. The new sovereign's first act was to surround his father's palace with soldiers, forbidding anyone, including his mother, to leave until he had searched all the rooms for his father's private papers. They were not there; Vicky had already sent them secretly to Windsor.

When Friedrich died, Queen Victoria consoled her daughter by writing: 'None of my own sons could be a greater loss. He was so good, so wise, and so fond of me.' Vicky's brother, the Prince of Wales, wrote to his son the Duke of York: 'Try, my dear Georgy, never to forget Uncle Fritz. He was one of the finest and noblest characters ever known; if he had a fault, he was too good for this world.'

The new Emperor sounded a brassy note in his first public proclamation: 'So we are bound together—I and the army—so we are born for one another, and so we shall hold together indissolubly, whether as God wills, we are to have peace or storm.' Puzzled Europeans turned to look at this new monarch. They saw a young man five feet nine inches tall, with curly blond hair. His proudest adornment was a bushy moustache with extended, upturned points, the creation of a skilful barber who appeared every morning at the palace with a tin of wax. '[The Emperor] walks into the room with the stiff stride of a Prussian soldier,' noted a British visitor. 'He speaks with a good deal of intense and energetic gesture. ...' 'If he laughs,' wrote another observer, 'which he is sure to do a good many times, he will laugh with absolute abandonment, throwing back his head, opening his mouth to the fullest extent possible, shaking his whole body, and often stamping with one foot to show his excessive enjoyment of any joke. ... He will continually shake the forefinger of his right hand into the face of anyone whom he wishes to convince or will rock slowly on his toes backwards and forwards.'

Wilhelm began his reign with exuberant gusto. Palaces were redecorated, new uniforms designed, and a cream and gold train ordered with twelve salon cars luxuriously upholstered in blue satin. Eventually there was an Imperial yacht, created by converting an old warship and painting it, too, cream and gold. Its name, of course, was *Hohenzollern*. Special blue envelopes carried mail from 'The All-Highest', as the new Emperor styled himself. When he entered a room, everyone leaped up, men clicking their heels, ladies dipping in curtsey. No arguments marred Imperial conversation; courtiers learned to bow and murmur: 'As Your Majesty commands.'

Wilhelm II had the temperament, if not the talent, of a major artist. He painted and wrote poetry, choreographed ballets and composed music, designed chapels, conducted bands, and preached from the pulpit. A serious student of archaeology, he went on digs all over Germany. To be close to richer troves, he bought the villa on Corfu built by Empress Elisabeth of Austria. His creativity found full scope in the design and wearing of uniforms; thus the German Army found its clothing redesigned thirty-seven times during the first sixteen years of Willy's reign. Berliners gossiped that the Kaiser put on his Admiral's uniform to visit the aquarium or to attend a performance of *The Flying Dutchman*, donned his uniform as a General of Engineers to dine at the Berlin Motor Club, and dressed in the uniform of a British Field Marshal to eat a plum pudding. Courtiers invited to hunt with the Emperor were appalled to discover that they were required to wear a new court shooting-uniform with high brown boots and silver spurs and a coat with a stiff high collar, which choked them as they hiked through the woods.

Wilhelm had streaks of meanness and crudity. Abnormally powerful on his right side, he liked to twist his rings inwards so that the jewels would bite any hand he was shaking. If the owner winced in pain, Wilhelm would laugh: 'Ha, Ha! The mailed fist! What!' Every July he took an all-male party aboard the *Hohenzollern* to cruise the fjords of Norway, tell dirty jokes, sing lewd songs, and indulge in adolescent horseplay. In the early morning the Kaiser regularly mustered all his guests on deck for physical exercise while he strolled among them, inspecting. He thought it especially amusing to catch a fat old man squatting and give him a shove that would send him sprawling. This same trait once caused grave diplomatic tremors when Wilhelm spontaneously pinched the King of Bulgaria's bottom.

The Kaiser's restlessness, vanity, and rapid swoops from exhilaration to despair kept his ministers in a constant state of apprehension. 'The Kaiser,' said Bismarck, 'is like a balloon. If you don't keep fast hold of the string, you never know where he'll be off to.' His furious scribbles in the margins of state documents—'Nonsense!' 'Lies!' 'Rascals!' 'Stale fish!' 'False as a Frenchman usually is!' 'England's fault, not ours!'—shocked only the few who saw them. But his bombastic letters, indiscreet conversations and sensational pronouncements sometimes reached a wider public. At various times Wilhelm described Queen Victoria as 'an old hag', the Prince of Wales as 'an old peacock' or 'a Satan', the King of Italy as 'the Dwarf', and the Queen of Italy (whose father was the King of Montenegro) as 'the daughter of a cattle thief'. 'I wish', his mother would sigh wearily, 'that we could put a padlock on his mouth.'

Whatever Wilhelm said or did Dona thought was wonderful. She loved, believed, obeyed and clung to him. The happiest moments of her day were the private breakfasts at which she could butter his toast and pour his coffee. When Wilhelm had finished, he jumped to his feet and marched away, shouting over his shoulder: 'Come along! No dawdling!' and Dona, whether she had eaten or not, hurried after him. Surprisingly, with all his restlessness and the pleasure he took in talking to beautiful women, there were no hints of infidelity. On this ground alone the submissive Dona might have rebelled. She was deeply

6 Emperor Wilhelm II.

religious—devoting her greatest effort outside her home to raising money for the construction of churches—and her morality was rigid. Young men suspected of sex before marriage were barred from court. The Prince of Wales had to be received, but Dona made plain by look and gesture that she considered royal birth no warrant for philandering.

Wilhelm's children, however, avoided him. When necessary, his only daughter, Viktoria Luise, could charm him into acquiescence, but his six sons dreaded his summons. He barked like a drill sergeant, laughed at their questions, and harangued them into silence.

Other Hohenzollerns fared no better. As head of the house, Wilhelm assumed the right to dictate every detail of their daily lives. He monitored their manners, morals, clothing, friends and whereabouts. Members of the house could not travel from one city to another without permission from the All-Highest. His nineteen-year-old sister Victoria was passionately in love with the handsome, thirty-year-old Prince Alexander of Battenberg, installed by the Russians as Prince of Bulgaria. Although Queen Victoria, Fritz and Vicky had enthusiastically supported the

7 Empress Auguste Viktoria.

match, Wilhelm forbade it, in defiance of his father's will, which had specifically stated: 'I charge you as a filial duty with the accomplishment of my desires.' Prince Alexander eventually wandered off and married a Viennese opera singer, Johanna Loisinger. Another sister, Princess Sophie, became engaged to the Crown Prince of Greece (later King Constantine I) and was preparing to convert to Greek Orthodoxy when Wilhelm, prompted by Dona, threatened extended banishment from Germany. Sophie converted anyway, and the Emperor relented.

Breaking the Kaiser's rules resulted in disciplinary measures. Hohenzollern princesses, Wilhelm had decreed, were not to leave their houses without both a lady-in-waiting and a gentleman in attendance. One day, Dona's younger sister slipped out to go skating on a nearby pond with only a lady as company. Unfortunately, she fell through the ice and had to be rescued. Wilhelm was informed, and within two days a member of his staff arrived with a letter addressed to the victim's husband:

> In spite of frequent admonitions, you have not been lucky enough to guide and keep your wife in the conception of life proper to a Prussian princess, which she has the high honour to be. I am, therefore, forced to use severe measures to make you comprehend that, in virtue of my office as Chief and Head of the Family, I have the power to insist on the observance of laws of traditions, decency and custom.
>
> Your court will be secluded from every communication from the outer world for fourteen days. You are to regard yourself as under arrest. . . . The arrest applies to your wife as well as yourself. I think fourteen days of quiet thinking will make clear to her that it is better to accommodate herself to the existing statutes. Wilhelm R.

The offending Princess took her revenge privately: 'The first thing I did was to climb on a chair and take down the only portrait of the Emperor we had, tear it to pieces and throw it into the fire. After that I felt decidedly better.'

With Fritz's death and Willy's accession, Vicky now lost the last shred of political influence. She felt her isolation keenly. 'Of course it would be far better for me to go away from Berlin and not return,' the Empress wrote to her daughter, 'but I cannot be banished from the spot where my darling husband and two sweet children lie buried, nor leave the house for good and all where we spent so many years together, and where now recollections haunt every nook and cranny. . . . Besides it would look as if I were afraid of them—William and Dona—if I gave up my rights.'

Throughout his life, Wilhelm's relations with his mother's homeland manifested his mingled feelings of love and hate for that country and its royal family. 'I adore England,' he once said to Theodore Roosevelt, and another time, looking at the Round Tower of Windsor Castle, he told an aide: 'From this Tower, the world is ruled.' The one monarch in the world whom Wilhelm truly respected was his grandmother. Yet before and after he became Emperor, Queen Victoria never hesitated to criticize his behaviour. 'The extraordinary impertinence and insolence and, I must add, great unkindness of Willy and the foolish Dona force me to say I shall not write to either,' she declared to Vicky at one point. 'As for Dona, poor little insignificant princess, raised entirely by your kindness to the position she is in—I have no words. . . . As for Willy, that very foolish, undutiful and, I must add, unfeeling boy, I have no patience with and I wish he could get a good "skelping" as the Scotch say.' A few months after assuming the imperial mantle, the Kaiser snubbed the Prince of Wales by refusing to make a scheduled state visit to Emperor Franz Josef unless the Prince, who was already in Vienna, would first leave the city. The reason, it turned out, was the Kaiser's fear that his uncle would treat him like a nephew and not like an Emperor. Hearing this, Queen Victoria erupted with indignant wrath; she wrote to her Prime Minister, Lord Salisbury:

This really is too *vulgar* and too absurd, as well as untrue, almost to be believed. We have always been very intimate with our grandson and nephew, and to pretend that he is to be treated in private as in public as 'His Imperial Majesty' is *perfect madness*! He has been treated just as we should have treated his beloved father and even grandfather. . . . If he has such notions, he better *never* come *here*. . . . The Queen will not swallow this affront. . . . He must be made to feel that his grandmother and uncle will not stand such insolence. . . . As regards the political relations of the two countries, the Queen quite agrees that these should not be affected (if possible) by these miserable personal quarrels; but the Queen much *fears* that, with such a hot-headed, conceited and wrong-headed young man, this may at any moment become *impossible*.

The Queen's exasperation, communicated to Wilhelm either in person or through private channels, usually had a subduing effect and never resulted in permanent alienation. When news reached Berlin in 1901 that his grandmother was dying, the Kaiser rushed to Osborne, insisting that 'no notice whatever is taken of me as Emperor and that I come as grandson . . . what I do is my duty, the more so as it is this "unparalleled" grandmama as none ever existed before.' His gentleness and tact at her deathbed and at the funeral surprised and impressed his relatives and the British public. 'I must help them with many things, I must give them advice,' he wrote back to Germany. 'They are so kind to treat me like a brother and a friend instead of like a nephew.'

It was his role as nephew of the Prince of Wales that the Kaiser detested most. Both men had formidable egos, and each resented the precedence accorded to the other, the Prince because of his seniority in age and leadership in fashion, the Emperor because, until the Prince became King, he was the senior in rank. Bertie could be cutting about his nephew—'William the Great needs to learn that he is living at the end of the nineteenth century and not in the Middle Ages'; 'Willy is a bully and most bullies, when tackled, are cowards'—and too often his remarks, like Wilhelm's, travelled far. The two men also countered one another in taste. Wilhelm was puritanically virtuous and had struggled to be manly in a Prussian manner, with the result that after great difficulty he had surmounted the handicap of his arm and become a superior horseman. After fifty, the Prince was too fat to sit on a horse and didn't care. He liked pretty women in bed as well as at the dinner table, and despite his flaws, or perhaps because of them, Bertie had become the darling of Europe. Nor did it help that the wife of each despised the other's husband.

One taste which uncle and nephew shared was their love of uniforms and of changing from outfit to outfit ten times a day. To expand their wardrobes, Wilhelm appointed Bertie Honorary Colonel of the Prussian Dragoon Guards, and Bertie made Wilhelm Colonel-in-Chief of the First Royal Dragoons. Victoria had given Wilhelm the rank of Admiral in the British Navy. 'Fancy wearing the same uniform as St Vincent and Nelson!' exclaimed Wilhelm at the time. 'It is enough to make me quite giddy.' And when the Kaiser came to London for the old Queen's funeral, Bertie, now King Edward VII, created Wilhelm Field Marshal in the British Army.

Wilhelm outlived two British monarchs, his grandmother and his uncle. His attitude towards a third, his cousin King George V, was genial and patronizing. '[Prince George is] a very nice boy [and] a thorough Englishman who hates all foreigners,' he said to Theodore Roosevelt, 'but I do not mind that as long as he does not hate Germans worse than other foreigners.' Towards Prince George's look-alike cousin, the young Tsar Nicholas II of Russia, the Kaiser's patronizing took on a domineering tinge. Attempting to drive a wedge between Russia and her ally France, Wilhelm wrote: 'Nicky, take my word for it, the curse of God has stricken that people [the French] forever. We Christian Kings and Emperors have one holy duty, imposed on us by Heaven, that is to uphold the principle of "By the grace of God". We can have good relations with the R.F. [Republique Française] but never be *intime* with her.' Wilhelm liked to remind Nicholas that it had been 'my good fortune to be able to help you secure that charming angel who is your wife', and he signed his letters in a chatty fashion: 'Ta, Ta. Best love to Alix from your devoted friend and cousin, Willy.' Meanwhile, behind his cousin's back, the 'devoted friend' was writing to the British Foreign Secretary: 'The Tsar is only fit to live in a country house and grow turnips.'

It was ironic that the Kaiser's mother was to die less than six months after her own mother and of the same disease that had killed her husband. Vicky's cancer had been diagnosed two years earlier, and when the Dowager Empress (now known as Empress Friedrich) told Wilhelm, he did his best to suppress the aggravation he always felt in her company. Near the end, King Edward VII came to visit his sister almost as soon as he had buried their mother, bringing with him English doctors who recommended more intensive doses of morphine to dull her pain. The German physicians resisted, and once again there was a medical confrontation across a bed. When his mother died Wilhelm repeated his performance at the death of his father, sealing the palace off and searching the rooms for the deceased's private papers. Once again, however, Vicky outwitted him. All her letters and papers had been sent secretly back to England in the luggage of Sir Frederick Ponsonby, King Edward's private secretary.

Wilhelm might talk about the Divine Right of Kings, but, in reality, the authority he wielded as Kaiser was more limited than that possessed by either of his fellow Emperors, Nicholas II and Franz Josef. His ministers handled this fact carefully, attempting by flattery to shepherd him past the Reichstag, which had the power to approve or deny many types of legislation. Prince von Bulow, the minister so adept at political manœuvre that his colleagues called him 'The Eel', was especially good at lathering his master in praise: 'Beyond question, Your Majesty is more gifted than any of your relations, male or female. Your relations, however, do not extend to you a respect commensurate with the brilliance of your qualities—quite apart from the powerful position held by the German Kaiser.'

Wilhelm wallowed gleefully in the presence of such sycophancy, and it inspired in him the kind of statement he made in 1901 to his uncle, King Edward: 'I am the sole arbiter and master of German Foreign Policy and the Government and country must follow me.... May your government never forget this.' This was not true, but once his mother was gone, no one remained in Germany who could break through the Kaiser's self-delusion and tell him so. In July 1914 Wilhelm, suddenly appalled that his bombastic encouragement of Austria had propelled his nation to the brink of war, tried to reverse his course and pull Germany back from the abyss. But he was not the sole arbiter, and his country did not follow him.

The Romanovs

'A sovereign whom she does not look upon as a gentleman,' was the way Queen Victoria once described Emperor Alexander III of Russia. The Tsar responded in kind: 'A nasty, interfering old woman' was his bouquet to the Queen. Victoria's aversion may have been grounded in politics, for in 1855, when she was thirty-five and Alexander a boy of ten, Britain and Russia had fought the Crimean War. Ever since, British diplomacy had stood as a barrier to Russian expansionism towards the Bosporus or the Afghan frontier and India. The Queen's disdain may also have stemmed from the Emperor's manners, since Alexander was gruff, blunt, narrow, and suspicious. He had strong likes and dislikes, favouring everything Slav and distrusting everything English and German.

In this uncongenial atmosphere, the strongest link between the English and Russian families lay in the two Danish sisters, Alix and Minny (Alexandra and Marie), who married, respectively, the Prince of Wales and the Tsarevich (or Crown Prince) Alexander, known to his intimates as Sasha. With his usual tact, Bertie soothed his mother's fears as he embarked upon a visit to Russia in 1879. 'I shall of course avoid politics as much as possible,' he wrote to her, 'but as he is married to dear Alix's sister, who I am very fond of, I am most anxious that our relations should not be strained.' In fact, Minny's marriage to Sasha had happened in a way that presaged the union of George V and Queen Mary. Originally Minny was engaged to Alexander's older brother Nicholas. But in 1865 Nicholas lay gravely ill with pneumonia at Cannes, and before he died—so the story goes—the Tsarevich called Sasha and Minny into his room, took their hands in his, and made them pledge that they would honour his memory by marrying. The wedding took place the following year.

It was a match between opposites. Alexander, born to the imperial pomp of the Romanov court, hated show and insisted that a true Russian should be simple in manners, speech and dress. He was the first Russian monarch since Peter the Great to grow a beard, and he wore his own trousers and boots until they were threadbare. His normal day began at dawn when he rose, washed in cold water, made himself a pot of coffee, and sat down at his desk. Later, Marie would join him for a breakfast of rye bread and boiled eggs. Alexander's idea of relaxation was to shoulder a gun and spend the entire day hunting in the marshes or forests.

Marie, born Princess Dagmar into the impoverished circumstances of Prince Christian's family, gloried in the magnificence of the St Petersburg court. The Empress, wrote the wife of the American Minister in 1886, 'wore the Russian court dress... of dark blue velvet very heavily embroidered with gold.... The sleeves hung nearly to the floor; the waist was partly blue velvet, partly white satin embroidered with gold, the petticoat of white satin was embroidered in front with gold. She had a *kokoshnik* [ancient Russian headdress] on her head—a velvet diadem covered with jewels, from which fell a beautiful lace veil. I saw on her neck a sapphire as large as a hen's egg. She looked lovely, and bowed and smiled in recognition of the deep reverences we all made.'

The dark-haired Empress delighted in parties and balls. 'I danced and danced. I let myself be carried away,' wrote Marie when she was forty-four. Her husband disliked dancing. Sometimes, when the evening had gone on too long for him, he would order the musicians, one by one, to pack up and leave. Finally, if his wife and the guests persisted in dancing, Alexander would turn off the lights. 'Well,' said the Empress with a smiling shrug, 'I suppose the Emperor wants us all to go home.'

Marie delighted in gossip and human frailty. 'They danced the mazurka for half an hour,' she wrote in one letter. 'One poor lady lost her petticoat which remained at our feet until a general managed to hide it behind a pot of flowers.' When the Archduke Franz Ferdinand, heir to the Habsburg Empire, visited St Petersburg in 1891, Marie reported with amused sympathy: 'He is so feted, he is stuffed with lunches and dinners everywhere so that he will end by having a monstrous indigestion. Last night at the theatre, he looked already rather pasty and left early with a migraine.'

Before she was thirty, tiny Marie had produced five children: Nicholas (who became the Tsarevich when his father ascended the throne), George, Xenia, Michael and Olga. She was close to her older children, but the younger ones found her distant. 'Going to her rooms was a duty,' recalled her daughter Grand Duchess Olga. 'I never felt at my ease. I could never bring myself to speak naturally.' Yet little Olga could climb up into the lap of the gruff giant who was her father and feel totally secure.

The eldest son of this bearlike Tsar and sparkling Empress was a slender young man, five feet seven inches tall, with blue eyes and a quiet, gentle charm. 'Nicky smiled his usual tender, shy, slightly sad smile,' wrote a male cousin of the Tsarevich. He was well educated. Thoroughly drilled in history, he also had a mastery of languages, speaking French, German and English as well as Russian. He rode beautifully, danced gracefully, was an excellent shot, and later became an enthusiastic player of lawn tennis. At nineteen, Nicholas commanded a squadron in the

Horse Guards and participated in the pleasant, mindless existence of all aristocratic young officers: 'Each day we drill twice . . . the dinners are very merry . . . after meals, the officers play billiards, skittles, cards or dominoes . . . we got stewed . . . tasted six sorts of Port and got a bit soused . . . we wallowed in the grass and drank . . . felt owlish . . . the officers carried me out.'

In the spring of 1890 Nicholas met a seventeen-year-old dancer in the Imperial Ballet, Mathilde Kschessinska, who purposefully set her sights on the Tsarevich. Her campaign took time, but eventually Nicholas pressed into her hand a gold bracelet studded with diamonds and a large sapphire and became a regular visitor to the small, two-storey house which she had rented in St Petersburg. Both understood that the liaison was temporary, and Kschessinska went on to other arrangements with various Grand Dukes and a career as one of the great ballerinas of pre-revolutionary Russia.

In 1893 Nicholas arrived in London to represent his father at the wedding of George, Duke of York, to Princess Mary of Teck. 'May is delightful and much better looking than her photograph,' the Tsarevich reported to his mother. 'Uncle Bertie, of course, sent me at once a tailor, a bootmaker and a hatter,' he went on. Wearing the latest styles, the Tsarevich pleased Queen Victoria because he looked not like a Russian but 'very like Georgie!' Indeed, so great was Nicholas's resemblance to his first cousin that it created some confusion. At a garden party the Tsarevich received warm congratulations while the British heir was politely asked whether he had come to London solely to attend the wedding or whether he would be doing other business as well.

A little over a year later Nicholas himself was married. In 1892, upon his return from a world tour, he had written in his diary: 'My dream is some day to marry Alix H. [of Hesse]. I have loved her a long while and still deeper and stronger since 1889 when she spent six weeks in St Petersburg.' Kschessinska was a young man's fling; Alix of Hesse was a royal Princess, the favourite granddaughter of Queen Victoria (and should not be confused with her aunt by marriage, Alexandra, Princess of Wales and later Queen of England, who among intimates was also known as Alix). She grew up in Darmstadt where her mother, Victoria's second daughter Princess Alice, had filled the palace with pictures and mementoes of England. An English governess, Mrs Orchard, ruled the nursery where meals included baked apples and rice puddings. In 1878 when Alix was six, diphtheria carried off one of her sisters and then—shatteringly—her mother. The old Queen often invited Alix's father, Grand Duke Louis of Hesse, and his motherless children to Windsor, Balmoral, and Osborne.

This tall, blue-eyed Princess with red-gold hair, German by nationality but impeccably English in language, taste and morality, first travelled to St Petersburg at the age of twelve to attend the wedding of her sister Elisabeth (known as Ella) to Grand Duke Sergei. There Alix met the sixteen-year-old Tsarevich Nicholas who gave her a brooch. Five years later, in 1889, she returned to Russia to visit her sister. Now Nicholas accompanied her to receptions, suppers and balls, and took her ice-skating and tobogganing. Before she left, Nicholas persuaded his parents to give a special tea-dance with *blinis* and caviar. When she had gone, he confessed to his diary that he was in love.

Nicholas did not find it easy to convince Alexander and Marie, who had hoped for a more substantial catch. But Nicholas was determined. If he could not have Alix, he declared, he would not marry. Alix, for her part, liked the gentle Tsarevich with his wistful charm and warm blue eyes. The barrier was his religion, which every new member of the Russian Imperial family had to adopt. She was a passionate Lutheran, and to reject a faith that she had sworn at the altar to accept seemed an insult to God. The dazzling title offered by Nicholas tempted her not at all. She had already rejected the proposal of Prince Albert Edward of England, who stood in direct line of succession to the British throne. (Ironically, if Alix had accepted Prince Eddy's proposal and Eddy had lived, then he and Alix, not George V and Mary, would have been King and Queen of England. And the haemophilia that Alix transmitted into the Russian Imperial family would instead have been bred into the sons of the British royal line.)

But Alix rejected Eddy, and even Queen Victoria, who had hoped the match would succeed, admired her granddaughter's decisiveness. 'I fear all hope of [Alix's] marrying Eddy is at an end,' wrote the Queen. 'She has written to tell him how much it pains her to pain him, but that she cannot marry him, much as she likes him as a cousin, that she knows she would not be happy with him and that he would not be happy with her and that he must not think of her. . . . This shows great strength of character as all her family and all of us wish it, and she refused the greatest position there is.'

Meanwhile, the Emperor Alexander III was having trouble sleeping. Influenza followed by kidney trouble brought him to reflect on his own mortality and on the fact that his son was far from ready to succeed him. Marriage seemed a path to maturity; Alexander and Marie reluctantly agreed that Nicholas should propose to Alix. The moment came in the spring of 1894 when the 'royal mob', including Queen Victoria, then seventy-five, the Kaiser, and the Prince of Wales, gathered in Coburg for the wedding of Alix's older brother. Alix still could not be persuaded to change her religion. 'She cried the whole time and only whispered now and then, No, I cannot,' Nicholas wrote to his mother. The Tsarevich then wheeled up heavy artillery. Queen Victoria spoke to her granddaughter, declaring that Orthodoxy and Lutheranism were not so terribly different. The Kaiser added encouragement. Finally, Alix's sister Elisabeth, who had followed the same path from Lutheranism to Orthodoxy in order to marry Grand Duke Sergei, advised acceptance. The following day, Nicholas wrote: 'We were left alone and with her first words she consented. I cried like a child, and she did too, but her expression had changed. Her face was lit by a quiet contentment.' A cousin recalled: 'I was sitting in my room . . . getting ready for a luncheon party when Alix stormed into my room, threw her arms around my neck and said, "I'm going to marry Nicky!"'

Empress Marie bowed to her son's decision. 'Your dear Alix already is quite like a daughter to me,' she wrote from Russia.

'Her letter has touched me deeply—only—I don't want her to call me "Aunty-Mama": "Mother dear", that's what I am to her now. . . . Ask Alix which stones she likes most, sapphires or emeralds?' That summer, the newly engaged couple spent six weeks together in England under the guardian eye of Queen Victoria. At Windsor the Tsarevich presented his formal engagement gifts: a pink pearl ring, a necklace of large pink pearls, a chain bracelet bearing a massive emerald, and a sapphire and diamond brooch. From the Tsar came the most magnificent gift of all, a *sautoir* of pearls created by Fabergé, worth 250,000 gold roubles. Shown this dazzling display, Queen Victoria shook her head and said: 'Now, Alix, don't get too proud.' The bride-to-be began learning Russian and an Orthodox priest came to give her daily religious instruction. In the afternoons, meanwhile, the royal lovers escaped to stroll in Windsor Park.

During their stay in England an English Prince was born. 'Yesterday at 10 o'clock a son was born to Georgie and May to the general joy,' Nicholas wrote. He and his fiancée became godparents to the baby, whom the world would eventually know as Edward VIII and the Duke of Windsor. It was at this time also that Alix began to write little messages in Nicholas's diary: 'Many loving kisses'; 'God bless you, my angel!'; and finally, 'I am yours, you are mine, of that be sure. You are locked in my heart, the little key is lost and now you must stay there forever.'

From this English idyll Nicholas returned to Russia to find that his father's illness had been diagnosed as acute nephritis and that the stricken bear had been sent to die in the sunshine of the Crimea. There the Emperor, aware of what was coming, refused to observe the diet prescribed for him. 'Baby dear,' he whispered to his sixteen-year-old daughter Olga, who sat by his bed, 'I know there is some ice-cream in the next room. Bring it here—but make sure that no one sees you.'

With his father growing steadily weaker, Nicholas urgently telegraphed his fiancée to join him. When Alix arrived, Alexander III struggled out of bed and into full uniform to receive her sitting in a chair—the only dignified way, he insisted, for a Russian Emperor to greet a future Russian Empress. Ten days later he was dead at forty-nine, and the guns of the warships in Yalta harbour proclaimed the accession of his twenty-six-year-old son. 'Sandro, what am I going to do?' the mourning, neophyte sovereign asked his brother-in-law, Grand Duke Alexander. 'I know nothing of the business of ruling.'

The embalmed body made its way through Moscow to St Petersburg where, once again, the 'royal mob' assembled. The Prince and Princess of Wales and their son, Prince George (the Prince of Wales had telegraphed his son to come, not only 'out of respect for poor, dear Uncle Sasha's memory,' but also 'because the opportunity to see the great capital of Russia is not to be missed'), Prince Henry of Prussia, the Archduke Franz Ferdinand, and the Kings of Denmark, Greece, Roumania and Serbia were there, along with hundreds of Russian officials, army officers, members of the nobility, and representatives of all the provinces and peoples of the empire. 'I have received so many delegations . . . my head is spinning,' said Nicholas. For seventeen days the body lay exposed in its coffin in the Fortress of St Peter and St Paul while thousands of people shuffled past. 'Every day, after lunch, we had another service at the church,' the Duke of York wrote to his wife in England. 'We all went up to the coffin . . . and kissed the Holy Picture which he holds in his hands. It gave me a shock when I saw his dear face so close to mine.'

Amidst the candles and black shrouds, Princess Alix, now converted to Russian Orthodoxy and given the new Russian name of Alexandra Feodorovna, was suddenly to be married. 'One's feelings one can imagine,' she wrote to her sister. 'One day in deepest mourning, the next in smartest clothes being married . . . a white dress instead of a black.' But a wedding always carries its own kind of triumph. 'She looked too wonderfully lovely,' George wrote to May. 'I think Nicky is a lucky man . . . and I must say I never saw two people more in love.' That night, before going to bed, Alexandra again wrote in Nicholas's diary: 'At last united, bound for life, and when this life is ended, we meet again in the other world and remain together for eternity.' The next morning, she added: 'Never did I believe there could be such utter happiness in this world, such a feeling of unity between two mortal beings. I love you, these three words have my life in them.'

The mingling of wedding and funeral, mourning and joy, produced much confusion of emotions and arrangements. Empress Marie, the bereaved wife, was the central figure in the drama. The Princess of Wales, sending her husband and her son back to England, remained in Russia for two months, sleeping in her sister's room as they had done as children. Nicholas had married so quickly that he had made no arrangements to house his bride, and accordingly the newly-weds moved into his mother's residence, the Anichkov Palace, where Marie ruled with an iron hand. Alexandra was ignored. 'I feel myself completely alone,' she wrote to a friend in Germany. 'I weep and worry all day long because I feel my husband is so young and inexperienced. I am alone most of the time. My husband is occupied all day, and he spends his evenings with his mother.' Even after the period of mourning was over, Marie, as Dowager Empress, took precedence over her daughter-in-law. Dressed in white and blazing with diamonds, she walked on the arm of her son while Alexandra followed behind on the arm of one of the Grand Dukes.

By the spring of 1895 the family strain had eased. Marie departed on a long visit to Copenhagen, and Alexandra discovered that she was pregnant. In November, when Grand Duchess Olga Nicolaievna was born, the young Empress nursed and bathed the baby herself, singing her to sleep with English and German lullabies. The following year, after his coronation in the Kremlin, the Emperor Nicholas II, his wife and child toured Europe, visiting the Emperor Franz Josef, the Kaiser, his grandparents, King Christian IX and Queen Louise of Denmark, and, finally, Alix's grandmother, Queen Victoria.

The Queen was at Balmoral, whence she dispatched the Prince of Wales to escort her guests from the harbour at Leith to her granite castle in the Highlands. When they arrived, thoroughly drenched by rain, the tiny, elderly monarch was waiting for

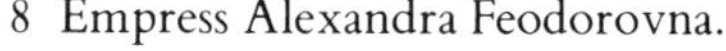
8 Empress Alexandra Feodorovna.

9 Emperor Nicholas II.

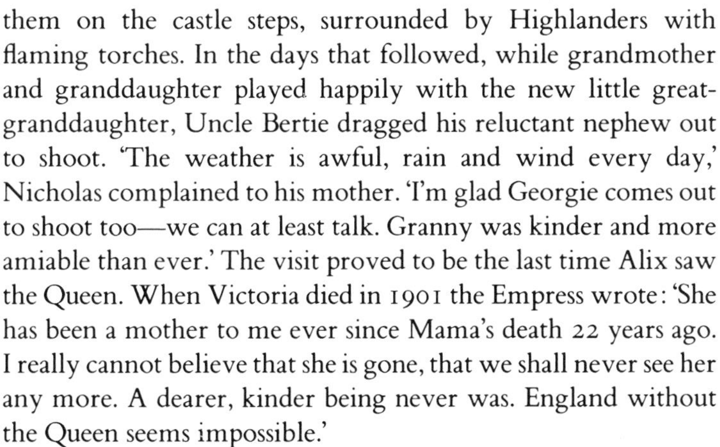
them on the castle steps, surrounded by Highlanders with flaming torches. In the days that followed, while grandmother and granddaughter played happily with the new little great-granddaughter, Uncle Bertie dragged his reluctant nephew out to shoot. 'The weather is awful, rain and wind every day,' Nicholas complained to his mother. 'I'm glad Georgie comes out to shoot too—we can at least talk. Granny was kinder and more amiable than ever.' The visit proved to be the last time Alix saw the Queen. When Victoria died in 1901 the Empress wrote: 'She has been a mother to me ever since Mama's death 22 years ago. I really cannot believe that she is gone, that we shall never see her any more. A dearer, kinder being never was. England without the Queen seems impossible.'

Three more daughters were born at two-year intervals, the names of the quartet—Olga, Tatiana, Marie, Anastasia—now making a sad litany of beauty, promise, and atrocity. Then, on 12 August 1904, Nicholas wrote in his diary: 'A great never-to-be-forgotten day when the mercy of God has visited us so clearly. Alix gave birth to a son at one o'clock. The child has been called Alexis.' The baby was christened in the presence of his eighty-six-year-old great-grandfather, King Christian IX of Denmark. Only six weeks later, Nicholas made a more sombre entry in his diary: 'Alix and I have been very much worried. A haemorrhage began this morning without the slightest cause from the navel of our small Alexis. It lasted with but a few interruptions until evening.' Soon after, the frightened parents received the terrible news: Alexis, like his English great-uncle Prince Leopold, his Prussian cousins and, eventually, his cousins, the royal princes of Spain, had haemophilia. In all these cases, the boys and young men and their families would suffer; in Alexis's case, all Russia and the world would feel the effects of the disease.

When Nicholas did create a home for his wife and family it was in the yellow and white Alexander Palace in the Imperial Park at Tsarskoe Selo, fifteen miles south of St Petersburg. The most famous room in the palace was the Empress's mauve boudoir where everything—curtains, rugs, pillows, chairs and couches—was mauve and white. Icons and pictures covered the walls, white tables and shelves were cluttered with papers, books, and objects in porcelain and enamel. Vases of roses, lilacs, and violets from the royal garden or greenhouse perfumed the air.

Here Alexandra spent her mornings propped up on pillows on a *chaise longue*, reading or writing letters. Here Nicholas, who always rose early, dressed by lamplight, and spent the morning at work, would come to take morning tea and discuss with his wife their children or the empire. Although he preferred to speak Russian with most people, the Tsar always spoke to Alexandra in English.

Here also the Empress would talk with her daughters, helping them to choose their dresses and plan their schedules. Most days they were drilled by tutors in arithmetic, geography, history, Russian, English and French. At eleven they stopped to walk in the park for an hour, sometimes with their father. In winter the Grand Duchesses skated on the ice of a large artificial lake within the park or sledded down piled-up mountains of snow. Family lunch was always simple. Although Nicholas employed an excellent French chef, his own preference was for basic Russian fare: cabbage soup or *borshch, kasha* with boiled fish, and fruit. Tea, accompanied by hot bread and English biscuits, was at four. The Emperor drank two cups, never more, never less, and then returned to his study, a small room with one window and plain leather chairs, to work until after eight. Following dinner the family sat together in a drawing-room, talking, reading aloud, or pasting snapshots and postcards into green leather albums stamped in gold with the Imperial monogram. Nicholas's day ended at eleven. After a hot bath he went to bed and usually to sleep, except when his wife, on the other side of their double bed, kept him awake, still reading and munching English biscuits.

On the floor above their heads, the children slept on hard beds without pillows and rose to take cold baths every morning. The girls were trained to work alongside their maids, making their beds and straightening their rooms. Olga, the eldest, had long reddish-blonde hair, a good mind and quiet wit and was closest, both in character and in feeling, to her father. Tatiana, slender with rich auburn hair and deep grey eyes, was the most elegant, energetic and purposeful of the Grand Duchesses. Her sisters called her 'the Governess'. 'You felt that she was the daughter of an Emperor,' declared a Guards officer. Marie, with red cheeks, thick light-brown hair, and blue eyes so large that they were called 'Marie's saucers', was the prettiest. She was also flirtatious, lazy, and so charming that her little first cousin Louis of Battenberg, who would grow up to become Earl Mountbatten of Burma, declared that at the age of twelve 'my dream was to marry her'. Anastasia, the youngest, was a mimic and a tomboy with a streak of stubbornness, mischief and impertinence. Generally secluded from other children, the girls became exceptionally close, proclaiming their unity by choosing a single autograph—OTMA—which they derived from the first letters of their names and used to sign joint letters and also to make joint gifts.

Alexis, their handsome little brother, was born with blue eyes and golden curls, which later turned auburn and became straight. He was high-spirited and happy, and only gradually did the effects of his permanent condition begin to restrict his life. He understood that he was heir to the throne, and at six he once dismissed his sisters by saying: 'Now girls, run away. Someone has just called to see me on business.' Nevertheless, like most boys, the Tsarevich liked toy soldiers, kept pets, and filled his pockets with nails, string and pebbles. Few Russians knew of his affliction. Pierre Gilliard, a Swiss who was tutoring Alexis's sisters in French, came to the palace almost every day for six years without ever being told the nature of the boy's disease. At times his visits to his sisters' classroom would suddenly cease. 'My pupils' mood was melancholy which they tried in vain to conceal,' the tutor later wrote. 'When I asked them the cause, they replied evasively, "Alexis Nicolaevich is not well."'

The family of Nicholas II were never completely free of worry about this mysterious disease, but the episodes of illness were scattered through a pleasant and familiar cycle of migration from one Imperial habitat to another. Winter always found them at Tsarskoe Selo, although for specific ceremonial occasions the family might spend the night at the gigantic Winter Palace in St Petersburg. In May they moved to a comfortable wooden villa with many stairs, landings, alcoves and balconies on the great Imperial estate of Peterhof. In June they cruised the fjords on the southern coast of Finland in the Imperial yacht. August took them to the hunting lodge of Spala, deep in the Polish forest. In September they went to the warm air and pebble beaches of the Crimea, and in November they returned to Tsarskoe Selo for the winter.

The Imperial train that carried the Emperor and his family from one of these places to the next was made up of luxurious, royal-blue salon cars with the double-eagle crest emblazoned on the side. The private car of the Imperial couple consisted of a bedroom, a sitting-room for the Empress done in mauve, a study for the Emperor with green leather chairs, and a white-tiled bathroom. For many years the danger of a terrorist attack forced the authorities to adopt the practice of having two identical trains travelling a few miles apart so that would-be assassins could never be sure which one the Emperor was using.

Nicholas possessed the finest yacht in Europe, a 5,557-ton, black-hulled beauty called *Standard*. Built in Denmark, with the graceful design of a sailing ship, she was propelled by coal and steam. A bowsprit encrusted with gold leaf jutted forward from her clipper bow, and three tall masts towered above her twin white funnels. Gleaming wooden decks were covered with white canvas awnings and lined with wicker chairs and tables.

The Kaiser, whose 4,000-ton *Hohenzollern* was smaller and less beautiful, openly proclaimed his envy of the Russian yacht. 'He said he would be happy to get it as a present,' Nicholas wrote to Marie after Wilhelm's first visit on board. The Dowager Empress was indignant: 'His joke . . . was in very doubtful taste. I hope he will not have the cheek to order himself a similar one here [in Denmark]. This really would be the limit, though just like him and with the tact that distinguishes him.'

In June 1914, only a few weeks before the outbreak of war, the *Standard* voyaged to the Roumanian Black Sea port of Constanza, carrying the Imperial family to a meeting with the Roumanian Crown Prince Carol, who was of marriageable age. Grand Duchess Olga, then eighteen, was considered a prospect, but the young woman declared herself fiercely opposed. 'I am a

Russian and I mean to remain Russian,' she declared. Alexandra supported her, and Nicholas promised that Olga could marry whomever she liked, providing the candidate was suitable.

The real joy of life on the *Standard* came when the yacht was used for nautical holidays, especially the slow meandering along the rocky coast of Finland every June. Protocol was relaxed, the ship's officers dined with the family, and the Emperor's children wandered freely on the deck amidst the crew. When young, each royal child was assigned a sailor who took care that his small charge did not fall overboard. As they grew up, the Imperial daughters danced both Russian and Western dances with the officers. When the ship anchored in one of the granite-fringed fjords, everyone went ashore to pick flowers, hunt for mushrooms, or wade in the cold, clear water. Afternoon tea was served on deck while the ship's band thumped out marches. In the evening a thoroughly relaxed Emperor played billiards in the lounge and smoked cigarettes with his staff.

These scenes made up the life of the last Tsar of all the Russias and his family until the afternoon of 2 August 1914 when the world slid over the precipice into the abyss. The Great War changed much, but not the private feelings in this family. Nicholas and Alexandra remained passionately in love until the end. In 1915, when writing to him almost daily at Army Headquarters, where he had permanently established himself as leader of the Russian forces, Alexandra still used private terms of sexual endearment. It was this warmth and closeness that sustained them in the icy winter of Siberian exile and in the ultimate fate that awaited them in the Urals.

The Habsburgs

The longest reign in the history of modern European monarchy was that of a sovereign who mounted the throne in 1848, as a slender, wavy-haired youth of eighteen, and who died in 1916, a bald little old gentleman with mutton-chop whiskers, still doing his duty, as he saw it, to God and his people. The sixty-eight years that Franz Josef, Emperor of Austria, Apostolic King of Hungary, King of Bohemia and five other countries, Grand Duke, Margrave, Duke, Count and Prince of dozens of other territories and provinces, occupied the Habsburg throne exceeded even the sixty-four years that Victoria was Queen of England. To find a longer reign, one must slip back two centuries to the time of Louis XIV, who ruled France for seventy-four years.

A reign of such length suggests stability as well as continuity, and Franz Josef's achievement in holding together millions of Austrians, Hungarians, Czechs, Slovaks and others who spoke a variety of Slavic and Turkish tongues was a political miracle—even if most of Northern Italy did break away from the Austro-Hungarian Empire. Ironically, Franz Josef's reign began amid political chaos. The revolutionary fervour which swept all Europe in 1848 had infected the Habsburg domains. In Milan, in Prague, in Budapest, the streets filled with crowds demanding new forms of national freedom. It was too much for Franz Josef's uncle, the foolish, kindly old Emperor Ferdinand, whom Lord Palmerston once described as 'a perfect nullity, the next thing to an idiot'. 'I am the Emperor and I want dumplings,' Ferdinand had exclaimed in a statement that has come to characterize his reign. Dumplings, however, were not enough, and in December 1848, after nine months of turmoil, Ferdinand had to step down. His abdication and the elevation of his eighteen-year-old nephew to the throne were the work of a passionate, iron-willed woman, the old Emperor's sister-in-law, Archduchess Sophie of Bavaria. From March to December Sophie, with the help of a few loyal generals and politicians, held the monarchy together until the uprisings could be suppressed. Then, when the time was ripe, she dressed in her finest jewels, sent word to Franz Josef's younger brother Maximilian to put on his best uniform, and summoned him to witness Ferdinand's abdication and Franz Josef's accession. 'The function ended,' old Ferdinand wrote in his diary, 'with the new Emperor kneeling to his Emperor and master, that is to say, to me, and asking for a blessing . . . then my dear wife embraced and kissed our new master. . . . After that I and my dear wife packed our things.'

Franz Josef's path to the throne was irregular, but once firmly seated he believed and acted as the Lord's anointed. The Habsburg monarchy was an autocracy, every bit as much as the Romanov monarchy, and Franz Josef saw the relationship of God, ruler and people as one of pure and simple hierarchy. 'I command to be obeyed,' the Emperor said to his officials and people, echoing what he assumed to be the Almighty's command to him. The work was sacred; its mission, to restore the authority of the crown and maintain the position of the empire in Europe.

From the beginning Franz Josef worked at his desk ten hours a day, but he was young and the times still allowed for play. A dashing rider, this Habsburg had also become an expert shot and a scrupulous parade-ground soldier. Moreover, he was a graceful dancer, and in his scarlet trousers and white tunic he made an elegant figure as he whirled the glittering ladies of Vienna beneath the blazing crystal chandeliers of palace ballrooms. Men as well as women succumbed to his charm. 'The young Emperor I confess I like very much,' King Leopold of Belgium wrote to his niece, Queen Victoria. 'There is much sense and courage in his warm blue eyes.' Sophie, eager for her son to marry in order to secure the dynasty, passed several princesses for his inspection. Franz Josef rejected them all—and then spotted one himself who was scarcely even of marriageable age. Elisabeth of Bavaria, his mother's niece and his own first cousin, had come to the Imperial retreat at Ischl amid the lakes and mountains to accompany her mother and her older sister. She was only sixteen, but the twenty-two-year-old Emperor was smitten immediately. Called Sisi by her family, she had thick dark hair, shining eyes, an oval face, and a sensuous mouth that could flash in an instant from dimples to a pout—all of which made her perhaps the most beautiful princess in Europe. But Sisi was still unformed, more enchanting child than dazzling woman, more boy than girl, ready to run with her dogs or to gallop her horses at breakneck speed through the fields. Confronted with Franz Josef's ardent proposal, she was bewildered and frightened. Young Elisabeth of Bavaria was romantic, passionate, and poetic, but here was a young man of flesh and blood who wanted to make her his wife. Weeping, she said to her governess: 'Yes, I do love the Emperor. But if only he were not the Emperor!'

Franz Josef married this wild creature in April 1854 and loved her devotedly until her violent death forty-four years later. Sisi's feelings were more complex. Her wedding night was a brutal shock, and the following morning Sophie addressed her at breakfast with questions which left her wide-eyed. In the early years Sisi wanted only to be with her young husband, but every morning before the sun was up Franz Josef rode away from their suburban palace of Laxenburg to his office in the great stone and marble Hofburg Palace in Vienna. Thus sixteen-year-old Sisi found herself alone with her mother-in-law and the austere strangers whom Sophie had appointed as her ladies-in-waiting. Sophie regarded this time as a period of instruction and Sisi as a sulky, stubborn child who must be trained, or if necessary, bullied into playing the role of a Habsburg Empress. The antagonism grew deeper, with Sophie insisting, Sisi weeping hysterically, and Franz Josef attempting to mediate. When the young Empress became pregnant, Sophie demanded that she show herself to the court. Sisi, hating crowds and ceremonies, horrified at what was happening to her body, refused. A daughter was born and then another, and Sophie, now declaring that her daughter-in-law was unfit to raise her own children, attempted to take them away. Open warfare ensued and reached a peak when in 1858 Sisi gave birth to an heir, the infant Archduke Rudolf. Not long after, something snapped in Sisi. When her duties as Empress were mentioned, she shook her head; when her children needed attention, she vaguely waved someone else into the nursery.

Elisabeth told Franz Josef that she needed freedom, sun, orange trees, warm night breezes, and magnolias. Queen Victoria, appalled to hear of the condition of the beautiful young Empress, offered the *Victoria and Albert*, and Sisi sailed to Madeira in November 1860. For weeks on the island she remained locked in her room, weeping and staring out to sea. She returned to Vienna in May 1861, but a month later she left again, this time for Corfu, where she stayed fourteen months. Thereafter, the Empress often sought refuge on the Greek island in the Adriatic, building herself an exotic palace and settling down to a serious study of the Greek language. She developed a mania for appearing thin, limiting her nourishment to a glass of milk or a single orange a day.

None of this made any difference to Franz Josef. He loved her, but he could not abandon his duty and come to her. His letters were shrouded in loneliness and melancholy. 'My dear, dear Angel . . . My Heavenly Sisi . . . My only, my most beautiful Angel,' he wrote. 'This is my last letter before we see each other again. I can hardly wait.' Invariably, he signed his letters: 'Your lonely Mannikin.' Sometimes Elisabeth responded: 'Do you still love me?' she asked her husband. 'If you did not then nothing else that happened could matter any more.' The Emperor leaped to his pen: 'But my only beloved, poor Sisi, you know so well how I long for you. . . . I rejoice to madness in the wonderful moment when I shall find myself with you.' One of these reunions resulted in the birth of a fourth child, the Archduchess Valerie, in 1867.

The long struggle between Sisi and Sophie ended in 1873 when the Emperor's mother died. Sophie's last years had been ruined by the execution before a Mexican firing squad of her second son, tall, blond, dreamy Maximilian, who had accepted Napoleon III's offer to make him Emperor of Mexico. Sophie had been enthusiastic at the thought that both of her older sons should be Emperors, and her promptings were eagerly seconded by Maximilian's high-strung, ambitious young wife, Charlotte, the daughter of King Leopold II of Belgium. Their reign in Mexico lasted less than four years. When her husband was shot in 1867, the twenty-seven-year-old Charlotte (or Carlotta) embarked on sixty years of widowhood wrapped in a blanket of madness.

Sisi's illness was less certifiable. Self-absorbed, sensitive, guilty, and depressed, she was as unhappy alone as with other people. Desperate to escape responsibility, she searched for illusion; desperate to escape herself, she sought anonymity. Her restlessness became obsessive. She walked for miles, rode her horses to exhaustion, and took up hunting in England and Ireland, terrifying her hosts by the recklessness with which she took her fences. Sometimes seaside strollers at Bournemouth or on Corfu saw her, a slender, beautiful woman sitting alone on the beach with a lace parasol staring for hours at the horizon.

Even in her fifties, the aura remained, and Sisi was able to create a roomful of admirers with a single smile. There were no lovers. She usually travelled solitary and incognito as Countess Hohenembs. The person closest to her was her daughter Valerie, who received passionate letters from the Empress proclaiming: 'It is only you I love.' Franz Josef never wholly despaired. At fifty-seven, he still was writing: 'My endlessly beloved angel, your dear letter gave me so much happiness for it was one more proof that you love me and that you will be glad to come back to us.'

Sisi did come back from time to time, although never for long and never physically, but she did not leave her husband completely alone. Instead, with the utmost delicacy, she arranged for him an unusual liaison. Katharina Schratt was an attractive, bubbly young actress at the Imperial Court Theatre who cared nothing for politics and who genuinely liked Franz Josef for the simple man he was. She cooked him goulash, baked him cakes, and sat with him to pass along the chatter of the city streets and the backstage gossip of the theatre. Katharina provided the homely domestic life that Sisi was unable to offer. When they were apart, the Emperor wrote to Frau Schratt addressing her as 'My dear gracious lady,' and signing himself: 'Your devoted, Franz Josef.' Curiously, he never took her to bed. Perhaps it was his feeling that if he pressed too hard, the bubble might burst. Or perhaps it was his life-long yearning for his distant wife.

On 30 January 1889 the Emperor and Empress happened to be together in the Hofburg Palace. Franz Josef had risen at four in the morning from his narrow iron bed and worked at his desk until just before eleven. The Empress was up at six-thirty to bathe, be massaged and combed, to breakfast, exercise in her gymnasium, and receive a lesson in Greek. But the morning was interrupted, the day demolished, and history redirected by a message: Crown Prince Rudolf, the heir to the throne, had killed himself in his hunting lodge at Mayerling in the heart of the Vienna Woods. And before taking his own life, he had shot a beautiful, seventeen-year-old girl, Baroness Marie Vetsera.

Rudolf had been everything his father was not: intellectually curious, socially accomplished, politically sophisticated, quick-witted, and unfaithful. His father barred him from all serious participation in government, leaving him only ceremonial appearances. In this capacity he had learned to detest Wilhelm II—'By the grace of God he is dumb, but also energetic and stubborn and considers himself the greatest genius,' Rudolf wrote—and to like the Prince of Wales: 'I would invite Wilhelm only to get rid of him in some elegant hunting accident . . . but I like to invite Wales. He's in fine fettle and wants to see everything, take part in everything. He's indefatigable. . . . Nothing seems to tire the old boy.'

Unable to do anything useful in government, Rudolf turned to the army, to hunting, to women. He had a wife, Stefanie of Belgium, but she was dull, ponderous, and apathetic. Other women found him brilliant and charming. Marie Vetsera had already been proposed to by a duke, but she wanted more, she wanted the pinnacle, she wanted Rudolf. 'He is mine,' the Baroness whispered to her maid. 'I know I have no right to say it. He may not even know I exist. But he is mine. I feel it in my

10 Emperor Franz Josef.

11 The opening of the Great Exhibition at the Crystal Palace, 1851. From left to right, Prince Albert, Empress Eugénie of the French, Queen Victoria, Emperor Napoléon III of the French. The Great Exhibition, the first of its kind, owed much to the keen interest and energy of the Prince Consort. The idea of international exhibitions was taken up enthusiastically by France, starting with the Paris Exposition Universelle of 1867, the first of a long series.

Great Britain

Britain, according to Winston Churchill, has always been at her best when ruled by Queens. Certainly, such a notion finds resounding affirmation in the long reign of Victoria (1837–1901), which coincided not only with the period of her country's greatest industrial advance but also with the zenith of the British Empire, so vast that truly the sun never set on it—until well after the old Queen's demise.

But however remarkable the achievements of Britain's empire-builders, life at court—following the gaudy reign of George IV (1820–30)—proved to be relatively modest in Victoria's time. While Prince Albert lived, domesticity was the keynote, and after the Consort's untimely death in 1861, the Queen entered a mourning period that would endure virtually to the end of her life. Withdrawing to her homes at Windsor, Balmoral, and Osborne, she was scarcely seen again in public until 1887, when Her Majesty emerged from seclusion to be acclaimed on the occasion of the Golden Jubilee marking the first fifty years of her reign. Another decade brought the Diamond Jubilee, and by the time the reclusive sovereign died in 1901, she had become something of a legend. No other British monarch had worn the crown so long—nearly sixty-four years—and through the marriages of her numerous children and grandchildren, Victoria had come to be known as 'the grandmother of Europe', with her descendants occupying an ever-increasing number of European thrones. She died at Osborne House on the Isle of Wight on 22 January 1901, her pillow held by her grandson, Kaiser Wilhelm II, with other members of the family gathered about.

Her worldly, amiable, much-travelled son and successor, Edward VII, and his beautiful Queen, Alexandra, were to preside over a court whose openness and brilliance could hardly have been more different from the stodgy propriety imposed by Victoria. The 'long Edwardian afternoon', which lasted but nine years, liberated London society to sparkle as never before (or indeed since). With their broad, even democratic interests, the King and Queen went everywhere and attended all the great events of the social calendar. They also travelled widely on the Continent, the King frequently visiting Biarritz, which he helped to bring to the pinnacle of fashion.

George V, who reigned from 1910 until 1936, was as different from his father as King Edward had been from Victoria. But while King George and Queen Mary went into London society, their first four years on the throne, before the outbreak of the Great War, proved especially rich in royal ceremonial. This interlude gave Britain its second coronation in less than ten years. It also, in 1911, brought the investiture of the monarch's eldest son, the future Edward VIII, as Prince of Wales at Caernarvon Castle, in a specially devised ceremony that had no precedent. Later that same year, moreover, the royal couple voyaged to India, where they were installed as Emperor and Empress in a great open-air ceremony at Delhi—the first and last time that a British monarch participated in such an event. The Maharajahs, Rajahs, and Nawabs of the many Indian states assembled from all over the subcontinent to pay homage to their Emperor, who held court—or *durbar*— according to the ancient traditions of Indian royalty. With the

12

12 Victoria, Albert and their nine children. L. to r.: Alice, Arthur, the Prince Consort, Bertie, Leopold (in front of him), Louise, the Queen with Beatrice, Alfred, Vicky, Helena.

14 The Prince of Wales (later King Edward VII) giving a light to his brother-in-law, Crown Prince Frederik of Denmark (later King Frederik VIII).

15 The Princess of Wales (later Queen Alexandra) reading in the saloon at Sandringham, around 1888.

13

13 Queen Victoria and Prince Albert.

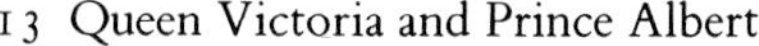

14

15

Princes arriving in a long procession of elephants, the sovereigns, dressed in coronation robes, sat enthroned on a covered dais. The Delhi Durbar has been described as the high-water mark of the British Empire.

If the British court holds a place of prime importance in Europe, this is owing not only to the long and often distinguished history of the monarchy, but also to the hard work, decency, and attractiveness of the royal family in the post-war era. Of the four Imperial houses, that of England was the only one to survive World War I, which swept away the ancient dynasties of Austria and Russia, as well as the relatively recent one of Germany.

16

17

16 Queen Victoria at work on state papers, Frogmore, 1893.

17 The Prince of Wales and Princess Alexandra of Denmark on their wedding day, 1863.

18 Queen Victoria at tea with Prince and Princess Henry of Battenberg (the Princess was her youngest daughter) and their children, Prince Alexander, Princess Victoria Eugenie (later Queen of Spain) and Prince Maurice, Windsor Castle, 1895. The Queen kept several Indian servants.

19 Queen Victoria with members of her family—almost all grandchildren—in the grounds of Osborne House, 1898. From left to right, Prince Leopold of Battenberg, Princess Marie Louise of Schleswig-Holstein with Prince Edward of York (later Duke of Windsor), the Duchess of York (later Queen Mary) with Princess Mary (later the Princess Royal), Princess Margaret of Connaught (later Crown Princess of Sweden), Prince Alexander of Battenberg, the Duke of York (later King George V) with Prince Albert of York (later King George VI), Queen Victoria, Prince Arthur of Connaught, the Duchess of Connaught, Princess Patricia of Connaught (fore-

ground), Princess Beatrice, Princess Victoria Eugenie of Battenberg (later Queen of Spain), Princess Helena Victoria of Schleswig-Holstein and Prince Maurice of Battenberg. Queen Victoria has been referred to as 'the grandmother of Europe'. She had nine children and forty-four grandchildren, most of whom married into the ranks of European royalty. Among her grandchildren were the Tsaritsa, the German Emperor, the Queens of Norway, Greece, Spain and Roumania, the Crown Princess of Sweden and the Grand Duke of Hesse and by Rhine.

20 Queen Victoria in about 1875.

21

22

21 A photograph taken in 1889 of Albert Edward, Duke of Clarence (right) with his mother Queen Alexandra and his younger brother, who became heir to the throne and eventually George V as a result of the Duke's death in 1892.

22 Princess Alice, second daughter of Queen Victoria, who married the Grand Duke of Hesse and by Rhine (the family was formerly called 'Hesse-Darmstadt') and whose children included the Tsaritsa Alexandra. She died from diphtheria while nursing one of her children who had the disease.

23 Queen Victoria in her drawing-room at Windsor Castle with her youngest daughter, Princess Beatrice. After the death of the Prince Consort the Queen depended on Beatrice to such an extent that the Princess was prevented from marrying until almost middle age. When she did eventually marry it was to Prince Henry of Battenberg; the couple remained in England where they brought up their family of three sons and one daughter.

23

24

25

26

24 King Edward VII towards the end of his life.

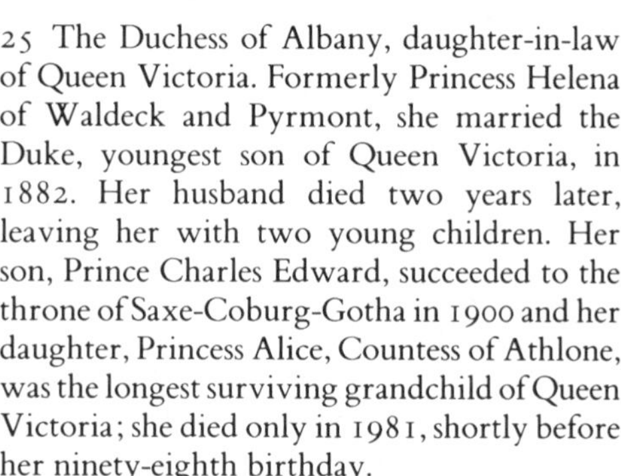

25 The Duchess of Albany, daughter-in-law of Queen Victoria. Formerly Princess Helena of Waldeck and Pyrmont, she married the Duke, youngest son of Queen Victoria, in 1882. Her husband died two years later, leaving her with two young children. Her son, Prince Charles Edward, succeeded to the throne of Saxe-Coburg-Gotha in 1900 and her daughter, Princess Alice, Countess of Athlone, was the longest surviving grandchild of Queen Victoria; she died only in 1981, shortly before her ninety-eighth birthday.

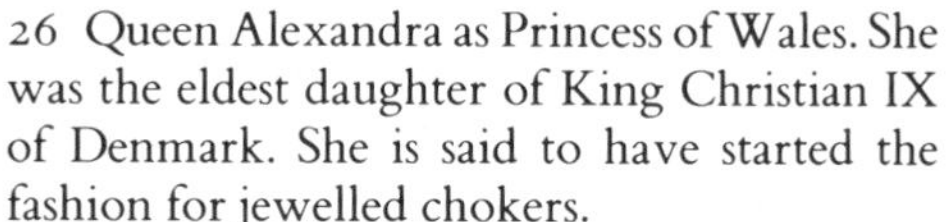

26 Queen Alexandra as Princess of Wales. She was the eldest daughter of King Christian IX of Denmark. She is said to have started the fashion for jewelled chokers.

27 Prince George (later King George V) on board Torpedo Boat No. 79, 1888.

28

28 The Duchess of Connaught, daughter-in-law of Queen Victoria, as Colonel-in-Chief of the 64th Prince Frederick Charles of Prussia Infantry Regiment. The Duchess, who was formerly Princess Louise Margaret of Prussia, married the Duke, third son of Queen Victoria, in 1879.

29 Queen Victoria draped with a fur rug, in the black silk widow's weeds and the little cap which she always wore indoors.

30 Queen Victoria's Diamond Jubilee procession entering Horse Guards, 1897. The seventy-eight-year-old Queen was reluctant to appear in public and had to be convinced that the people were anxious to express their affection for her. She did indeed receive tremendous acclaim and this great occasion marked the zenith of her long reign.

31

32

31 A charming picture of Queen Victoria in extreme old age, wearing spectacles.

32 Queen Alexandra (right) and her sister, the Dowager Empress Marie Feodorovna of Russia (who lived until 1928), on board the Royal Yacht *Victoria and Albert* in 1906.

33 Queen Victoria's funeral procession passing through the streets of Windsor, January 1901. The buildings are draped in black and hung with wreaths.

LONDON AND COUNTY BANK

34 The future Edward VII, in Prussian uniform, visiting a regiment with his nephew, Emperor Wilhelm II, in Berlin, 1890. Edward and Wilhelm did not get on.

35 King Edward VII and Queen Alexandra riding through the streets of London in the state coach on the day of their coronation, 9 August 1902. The original date of the coronation a few months earlier had had to be cancelled at the last moment as the King had fallen ill with appendicitis.

36 King Edward VII and Queen Alexandra with their daughter and grandchildren at Sandringham, 1901, the year of their accession. From left to right, Princess Victoria, Princess Mary, Prince Albert (later King George VI), the Queen, Prince Henry (later Duke of Gloucester), Prince Edward (later King Edward VIII) and the King.

36

37 The Prince and Princess of Wales (later King George V and Queen Mary) on elephants during their first visit to India, 1905. Riding with the Prince in the howdah is the Maharajah of Gwalior. The Princess of Wales is shaded by two umbrellas, one to protect her from the sun and another, according to eastern custom, to denote her royal status.

38

38 The Prince of Wales (later King George V) being handed a gun during a shoot, about 1906.

39 King Edward VII and his son, the Prince of Wales, in Highland dress. The King is smoking a characteristic cigar.

40 King Edward VII presiding over a tea-table at Sandringham. From left to right, the Countess of Macclesfield, the King, Miss Charlotte Knollys and M. Jean de Reszke.

39

40

41 The Prince of Wales (later George V, right) with his cousin, Emperor Nicholas II of Russia, at Barton Manor, 1909. Their mothers were sisters, and they resembled each other so closely that one was sometimes mistaken for the other.

42 King Edward VII on holiday at Biarritz, 1909. The King's regular visits to the French resort did a great deal to enhance its popularity and the people of the town had considerable affection for him.

43 Queen Alexandra, seated next to Sir Dighton Probyn, on the scenic railway at the White City, 1908. She paid 6d. for her ride, like anyone else.

41

42

44 The funeral procession of King Edward VII nearing Hyde Park Corner, May 1910. Nine sovereigns followed the coffin: as well as George V, there were the German Emperor Wilhelm II, Alfonso XIII of Spain, Frederik VIII of Denmark, Haakon VII of Norway, Ferdinand I of Bulgaria, Manoel I of Portugal, Gustaf V of Sweden, Albert I of the Belgians; President Roosevelt and M. Pichon of France also attended, and Archduke Franz Ferdinand of Austria.

45 The lying-in-state of King Edward VII in the Throne Room of Buckingham Palace, May 1910. King Edward's funeral saw one of the last gatherings of the kings and queens of Europe before the Great War.

45

Russia

In the early years of this century the Russian court was, without doubt, the grandest in Europe. According to Prince Christopher of Greece, whose mother, Queen Olga, had been born into the Russian Imperial family, 'there was something barbaric in its splendour, derived in part from the ancient Byzantine empire and evoking glories of the time of Catherine the Great and of France of the eighteenth century.'

St Petersburg, the Baltic capital with a 'window on the West' founded by Peter the Great in 1703, provided the sumptuous setting for the great ceremonies of state, except the coronation, which continued to be held at the Kremlin in Moscow. On such occasions the jewels worn by the Grand Duchesses always seemed more magnificent than those of other European royalty, no doubt because the Imperial family had access to the finest stones mined in the vast Russian empire. Along with moving his capital westward, Peter the Great (r. 1682–1725) forced his largely medieval and Oriental nation to assume a more Western character, not only in architecture but in dress and customs as well. Following this Tsar's reign, however, Russians reverted to their native conservatism, with the result that eighteenth-century ceremonial survived at St Petersburg in a purer form than at any other court. Russian Grand Duchesses still went to their weddings in ermine-lined robes of state and crowns set upon hair dressed in eighteenth-century ringlets.

The Kremlin saw its last coronation in 1896, when Nicholas II and Alexandra Feodorovna ascended the Imperial throne. The next day some half a million people assembled in the Khodynka Field, normally used for military manoeuvres, to receive souvenir cups and to catch a glimpse of the new Emperor and Empress, then only twenty-six and twenty-two respectively. When refreshment wagons arrived, great throngs rushed forward, causing many people to be trampled to death as they fell into trenches used for military purposes. The coronation tragedy now seems a portent of all that would follow.

Nicholas had married Princess Alix of Hesse and by Rhine, granddaughter of Queen Victoria, shortly after his father's premature death. The young Empress produced four healthy daughters before the birth in 1904 of the Imperial couple's first son and last child. The parents' joy over the arrival of an heir soon turned into anxiety when the Tsarevich Alexis was discovered to have haemophilia. Europe's best doctors soon arrived in St Petersburg, but they could do little since contemporary medicine offered neither treatment nor cure for the disease.

The desperate parents contrived to keep the Tsarevich's fragility from the Russian

52 The coronation of Emperor Nicholas II and Empress Alexandra Feodorovna, 23 May 1896. Although St Petersburg was the capital it was customary for the Tsar and Tsaritsa to be crowned in Moscow. This was, of course, the last coronation ever to take place in Russia.

people. Alexandra had always had a mystical streak, which only deepened with her conversion to Eastern Orthodoxy. Indeed, the Empress's religious zeal dismayed even the devout members of the court, who felt that the Imperial family were becoming progressively distant and reclusive. What drew them away was the evident power of Rasputin, a bearded peasant priest, to bring miraculous relief to the child's suffering. Despite pleas from many members of the family, including the Empress's own sister, Grand Duchess Elisabeth Feodorovna, the Imperial couple kept Rasputin in evidence, thereby tolerating his attempts to influence every aspect of their lives as well as the policies of the empire. Although well-meaning, Nicholas was weak and ill-equipped to hold together an immense land in the grip of war and revolution. In 1916, during his absence at the front, Rasputin was murdered in St Petersburg at the home of Prince Felix Youssoupov. Dissension in the army, a succession of military defeats, alienation from a devoted people, and scandal at court culminated in the Tsar's abdication in 1917 and the installation of the provisional government of Alexander Kerensky. At first kept under humiliating arrest at Tsarskoe Selo, the Imperial family were moved from place to place following the overthrow of Kerensky by the Bolsheviks. Their journey ended in Ekaterinburg, a small Siberian town, where Nicholas, Alexandra, and their five children were brutally murdered in history's most shocking regicide. In the same year, 1918, eleven other members of the Imperial family were assassinated, which brought a sudden and terrifying end to the Russian court, a world grander and more exotic than anything known elsewhere in Europe and ultimately the victim of forces beyond its command.

53

53 Nicholas, the Tsarevich, and Alexandra, Princess Alix of Hesse and by Rhine, about the time of their engagement in 1894.

54 Grand Duchess Alexandra Josifovna (seated left) with the Duchess of Connaught (daughter-in-law of Queen Victoria) at the coronation ball at Moscow. Behind, from left to right, are Grand Duchess Vera Constantinovna, Grand Duchess Anastasia Mihailovna, Grand Duchess Marie Pavlovna (the elder), Grand Duchess Helen Vladimirovna, Grand Duchess Elisabeth Mavrikievna and Crown Princess Victoria of Sweden, and in the foreground, Duchess Elsa of Württemberg. The attendant pages behind are members of the Corps des Pages.

54

56

55

57

55 The Emperor's eldest daughters, Olga (left) and Tatiana.

56 Grand Duchess Anastasia Mihailovna in Russian fancy dress, 1905. The only daughter of Grand Duke Michael Nicolaievich (son of Nicholas I), she later married Grand Duke Friedrich Franz III of Mecklenburg-Schwerin. Their daughter Cecilie became Crown Princess of Prussia.

57 Grand Duke Alexis Alexandrovich, fourth son of Emperor Alexander II, in fancy dress.

58 King Chulalongkorn of Siam in Russia, 1896. Seated, from left to right, are Grand Duchess Olga Alexandrovna (the Emperor's sister), King Chulalongkorn, Dowager Empress Marie Feodorovna, Emperor Nicholas II and Crown Prince (later King) Vajiravudh of Siam; behind, second from left, is the Dowager Empress's uncle, Prince Hans of Schleswig-Holstein-Sonderburg-Glücksburg, and at the far right, Prince Chiraprawat Voradej of Siam. King Chulalongkorn made two visits to Europe, where he had a warm reception at many of the courts, and Emperor Nicholas, when Tsarevich, paid a visit to Bangkok *en route* to Japan.

59 The Emperor's brother and sister, Grand Duke Michael Alexandrovich and Grand Duchess Olga Alexandrovna, on board the Imperial Yacht, HIMS *Standard*.

60

61

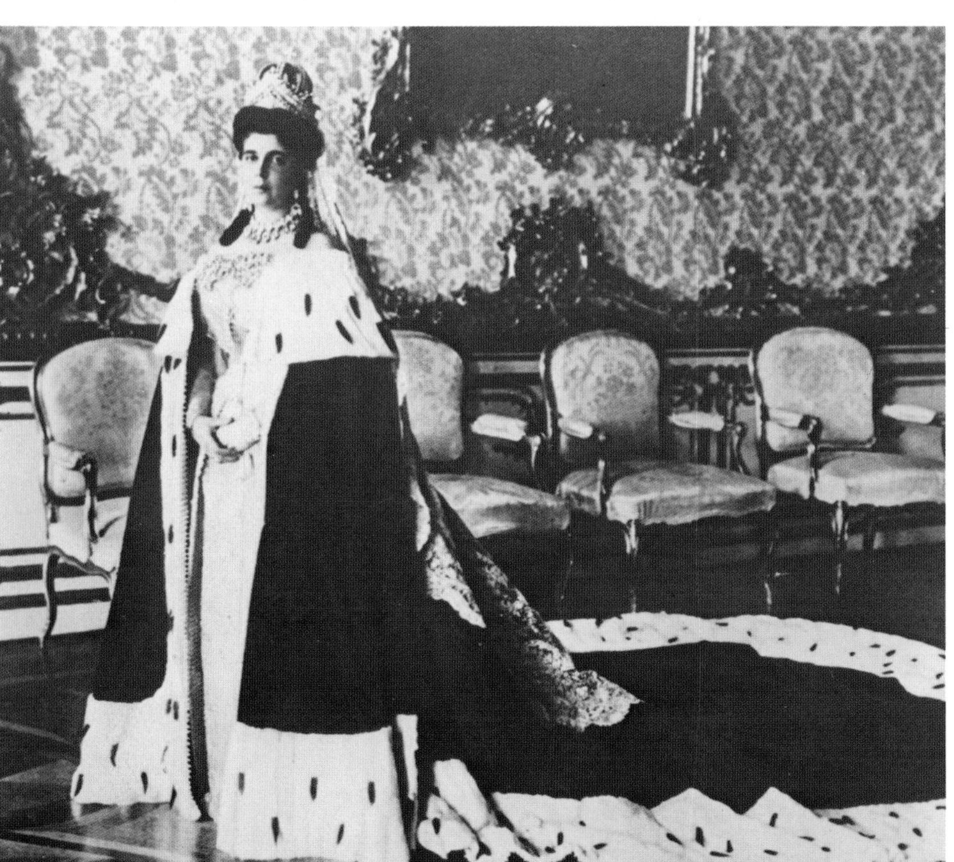

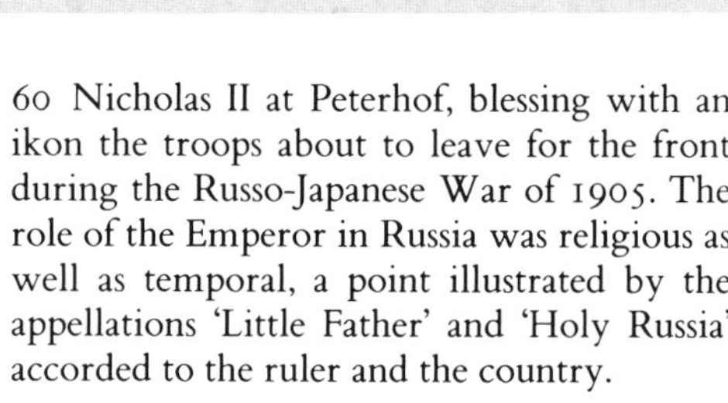

60 Nicholas II at Peterhof, blessing with an ikon the troops about to leave for the front during the Russo-Japanese War of 1905. The role of the Emperor in Russia was religious as well as temporal, a point illustrated by the appellations 'Little Father' and 'Holy Russia' accorded to the ruler and the country.

61 Grand Duchess Helen Vladimirovna, first cousin of the Emperor, on the day of her marriage to Prince Nicholas of Greece, 29 August 1902. It was customary for Imperial brides to wear a crown and tiara, and a heavy diamond necklace (which formed part of the crown jewels), as well as an ermine-lined mantle and a wig in the style of the eighteenth century. The robes were so heavy that the bride often had to be helped to her feet after kneeling during the marriage service. The wedding crown which can be seen in this picture was sold by the Russian government during the 1920s and is now at the Smithsonian Institution, Washington.

62

62 Emperor Nicholas II, Empress Alexandra Feodorovna and Dowager Empress Marie Feodorovna arriving at the Throne Room of the Winter Palace, St Petersburg, for the state opening of the Duma (Parliament), 10 May 1906.

63

64

65

63 The Emperor and Empress with their five children, photographed with members of the Tarnovsky Regiment, 1906.

64 The Empress posing for a sculptor.

65 The Emperor paddling in a canoe in the Gulf of Finland, where the family generally spent the summer.

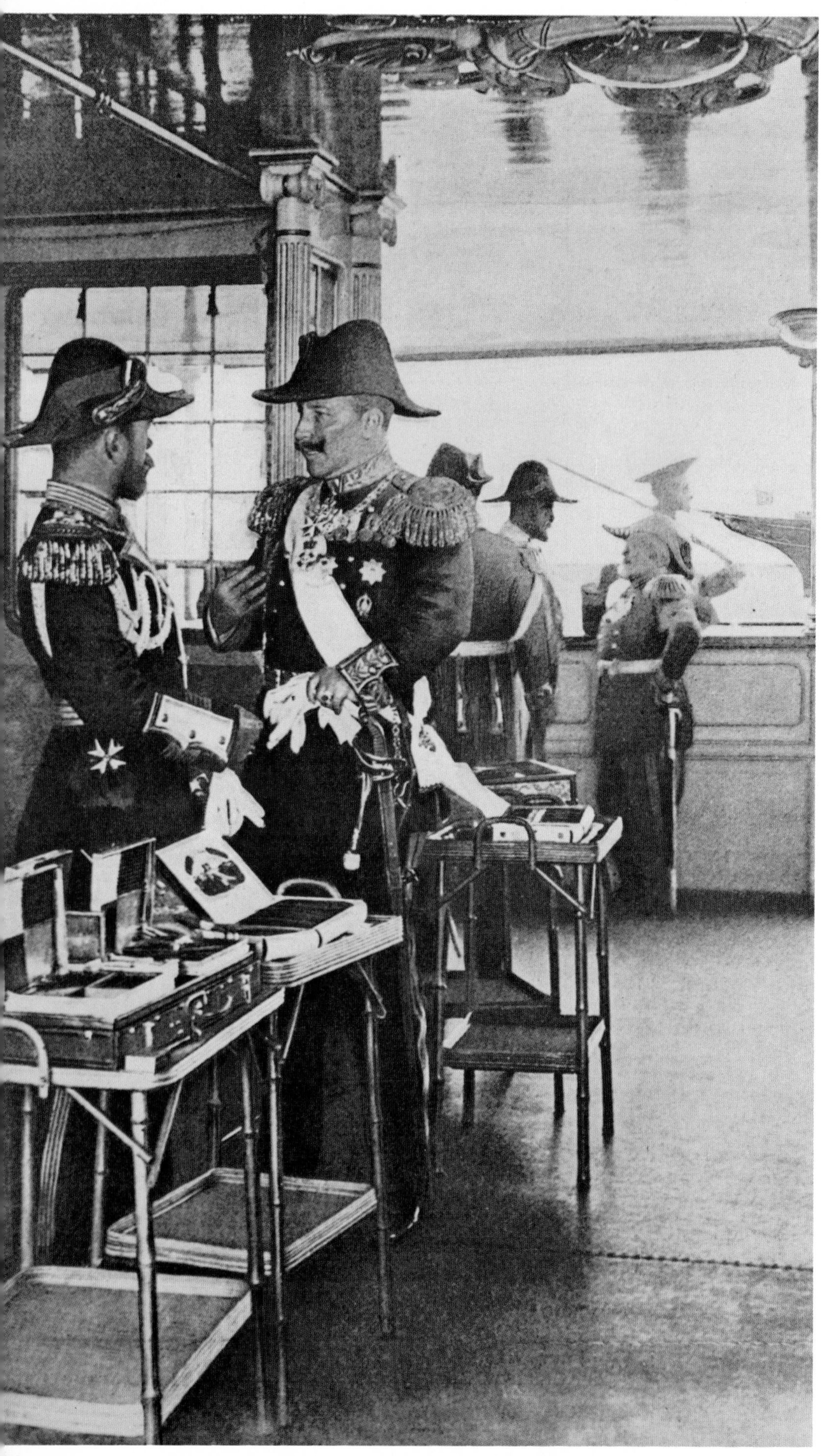

66 Emperor Nicholas II (left) and Emperor Wilhelm II about to choose cigars on board the German Imperial yacht, HIMS *Hohenzollern*, 1907.

67 Emperor Nicholas II with the Empress, his mother, the Dowager Empress Marie Feodorovna, and other members of the Imperial Family at the inauguration of the statue of his father Alexander III, in the Snamiensky Square, St Petersburg, 1909. The statue was sculpted by Prince Troubetskoy.

68

69

70

68 Grand Duchess Vera Constantinovna (Duchess Eugen of Württemberg), a first cousin of Alexander III, with her twin daughters, Duchess Elsa (left) and Duchess Olga, photographed on the occasion of the coronation ball in Moscow, May 1896.

69 Grand Duchess Marie Pavlovna (the younger), a first cousin of the Emperor, in court dress, with Prince Wilhelm of Sweden on the eve of their wedding in 1908.

70 The Emperor's children: left to right, Tatiana, Marie, Anastasia, Olga and the Tsarevich Alexis. The Grand Duchesses are wearing pearl-lined *kokoshniks*, a form of headdress much favoured at court, the style of which was derived from traditional Russian peasant dress.

71 The Emperor's two eldest daughters, Grand Duchesses Olga Nicolaievna and Tatiana Nicolaievna, about to set off for a military parade at Peterhof. Olga wears the uniform of Colonel-in-Chief of the Elisabethgrad Hussars and Tatiana that of Colonel-in-Chief of the Vossnessensk Lancers. It was customary for each Grand Duchess to be made Colonel-in-Chief of a regiment at her birth—there was only one exception, that of Olga Constantinovna (later Queen Olga of the Hellenes), who was made commander of a battleship.

72 Emperor Nicholas II (left) and General Joffre at a military review at Krasnoe Selo, 1913.

73 The Emperor and the Tsarevich Alexis in the grounds of Tsarskoe Selo, 1914.

74 The state coach, bearing the Tsarevich Alexis Nicolaievich in the arms of the Grand Mistress of the Court, Princess Galitzine, on its way to the chapel at Peterhof for his christening in August 1904.

75

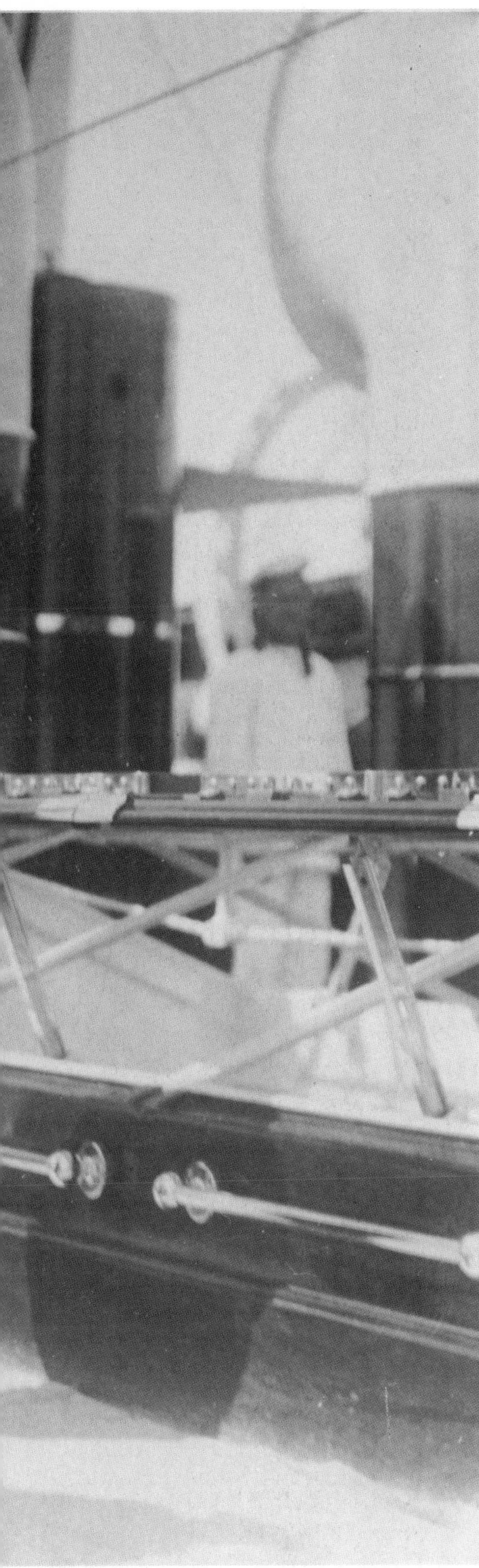

76

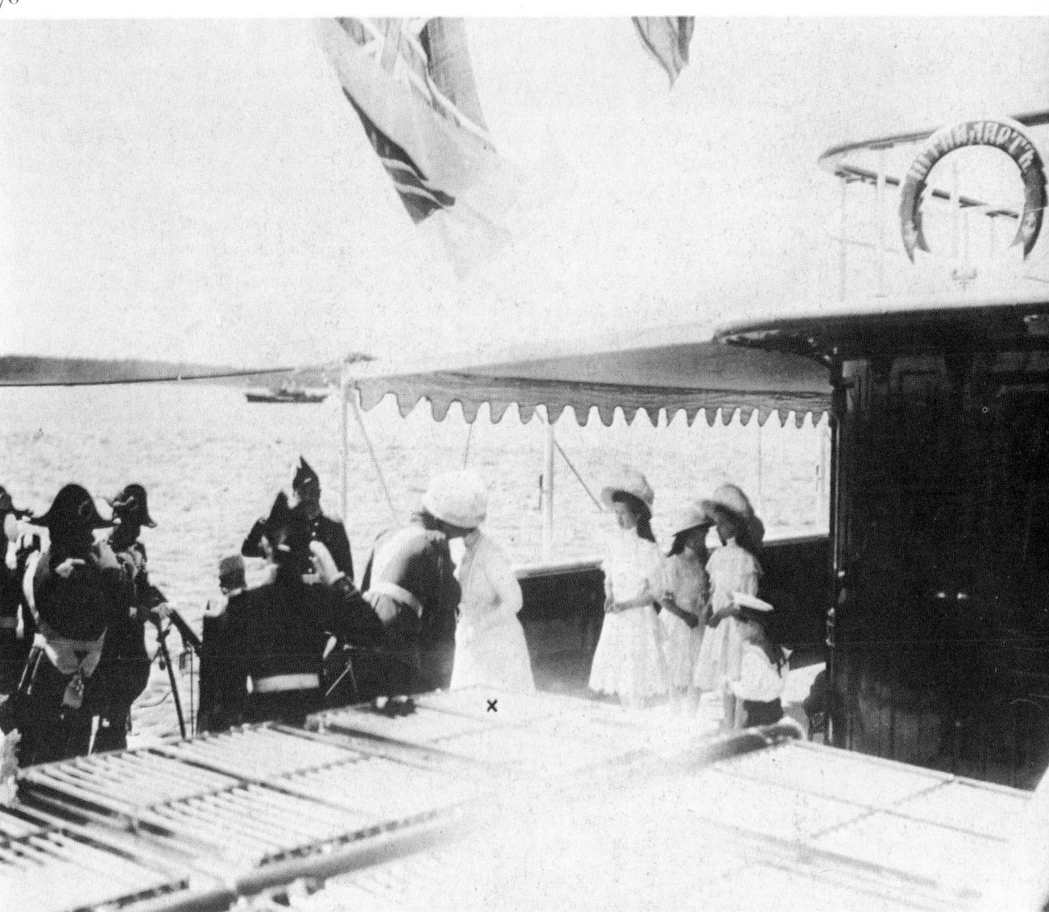

77

75 The Tsarevich Alexis being offered tea by one of the crew of the Imperial yacht, 1912. Behind him is Admiral Chagin.

76 Empress Alexandra Feodorovna greeting Emperor Wilhelm II aboard the Imperial yacht during the German Emperor's visit to the Gulf of Finland, 1909. Four of her children stand behind her.

77 The four daughters of the Emperor: Grand Duchesses Olga, Tatiana, Marie and Anastasia during a public appearance, 1909.

78 Rasputin taking tea with a group of society ladies in a St Petersburg drawing-room, about 1914. Rasputin was much feted by certain members of the aristocracy. Apart from the Emperor and the Empress, and the two Montenegrin wives of Grand Duke Peter Nicolaievich and Grand Duke Nicholas Nicolaievich, who had 'discovered' him, however, he had no contacts with any other members of the Imperial Family, most of whom strongly disapproved of him.

79 Empress Alexandra Feodorovna and the Tsarevich Alexis, during one of his frequent illnesses.

80 The Tsarevich Alexis playing with his sister, Grand Duchess Anastasia Nicolaievna.

79

80

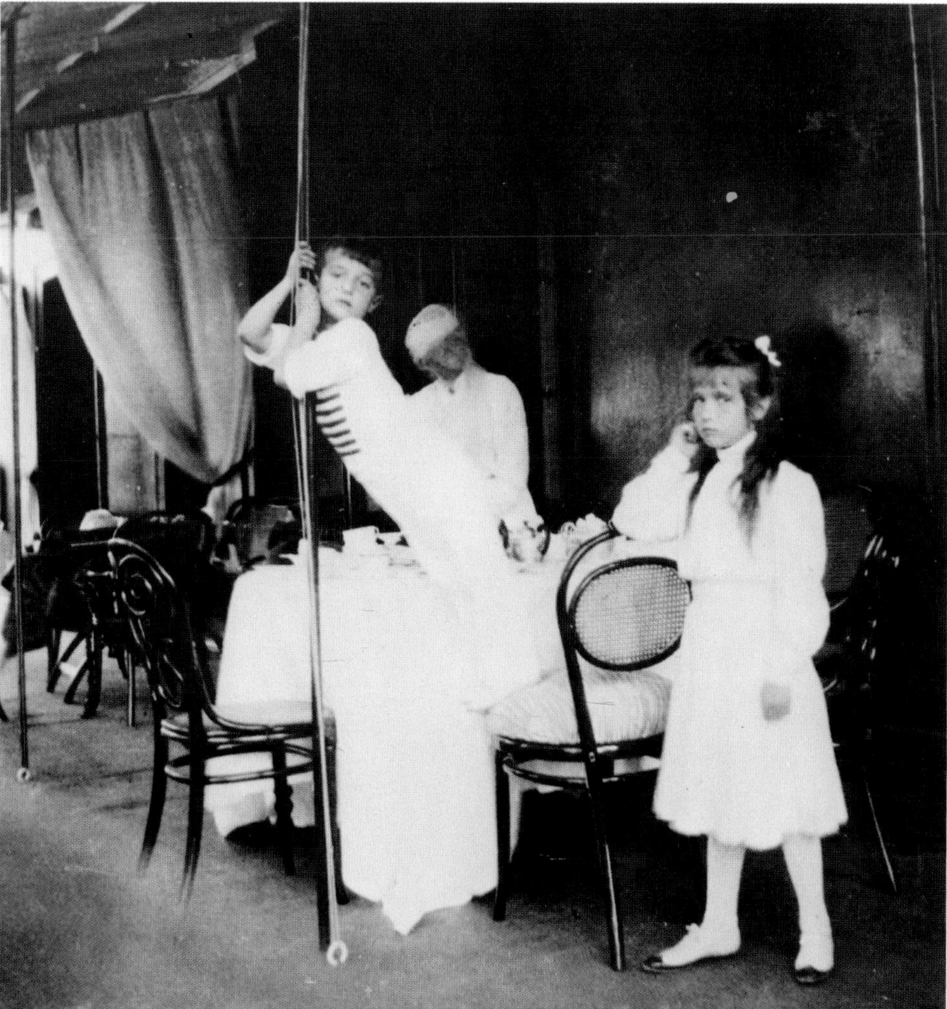

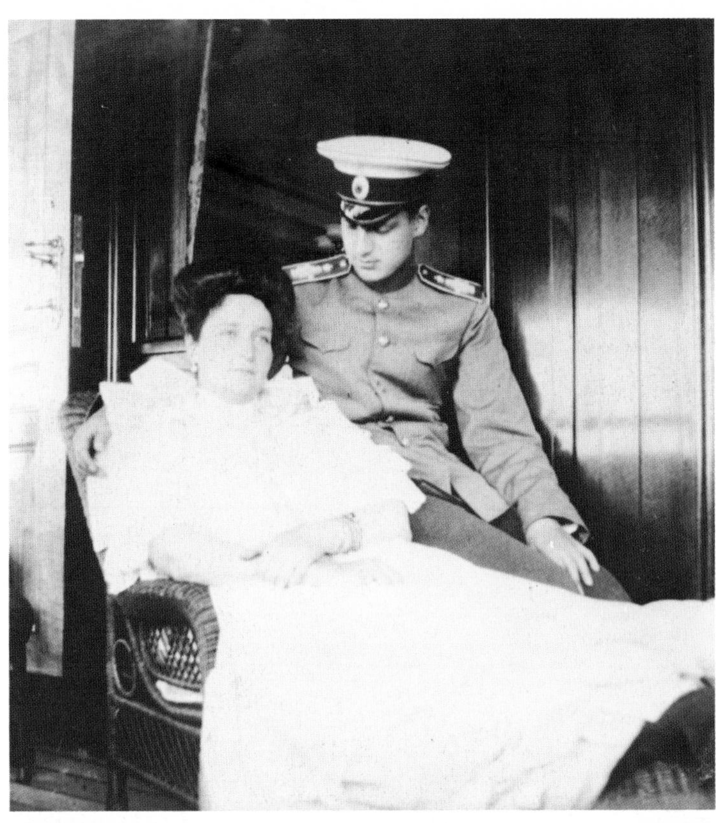

81

81 The Empress with her nephew by marriage, Grand Duke Dimitri Pavlovich. After the early death of the Grand Duke's mother, the Empress took a personal interest in his upbringing. It was thus particularly shocking for her to be informed that Grand Duke Dimitri was one of the three assassins of Rasputin.

82 A quiet domestic moment for Nicholas and Alexandra on board the Imperial yacht, HIMS *Standard*.

82

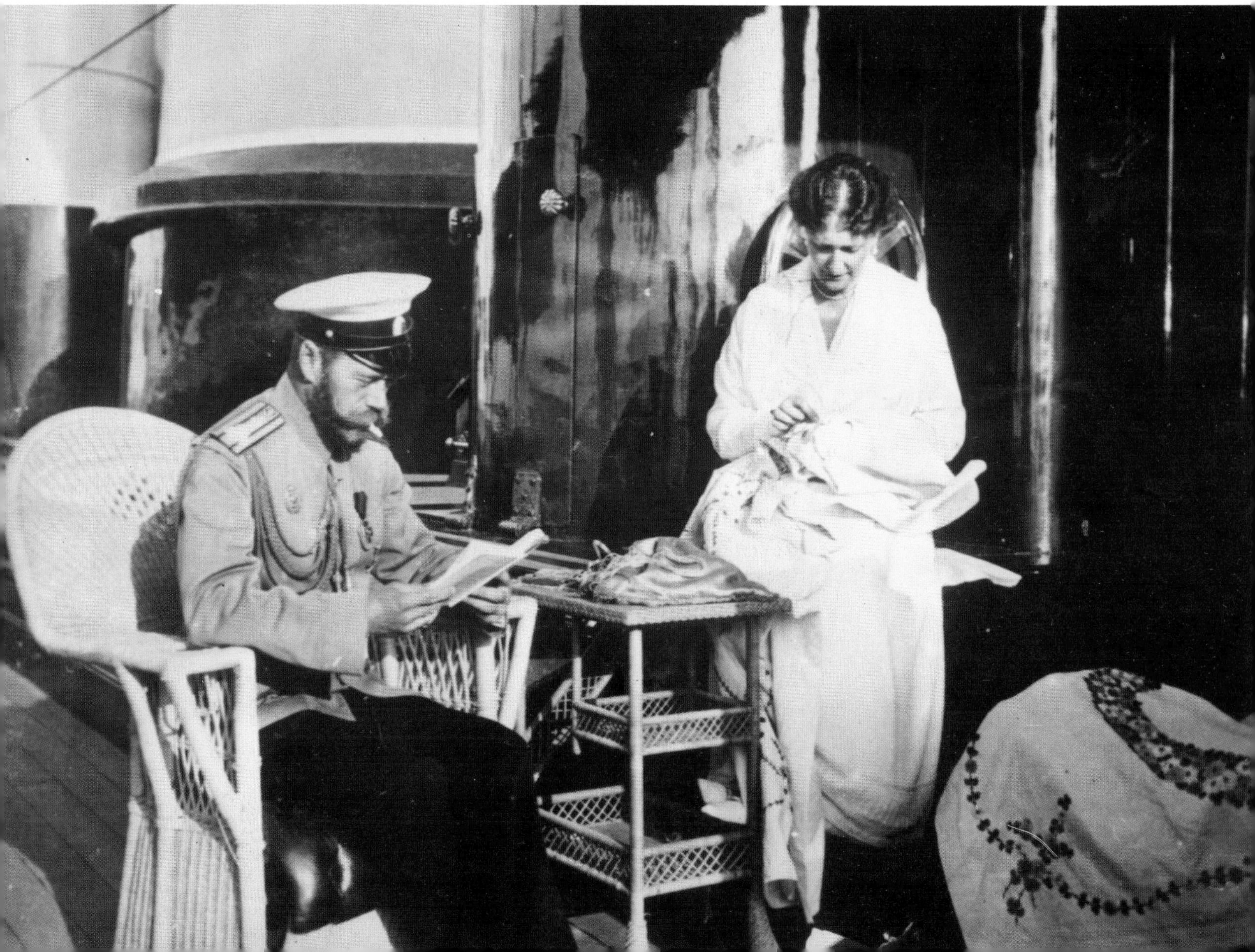

83 The Tsarevich Alexis Nicolaievich on his tricycle. The Emperor and Empress were constantly faced with the dilemma of deciding which activities to allow their energetic and high-spirited son, whose illness necessitated constant vigilance to prevent the least scratch or bruising. It is interesting to note that he was allowed to ride a tricycle, but it is doubtful whether he would ever have had a bicycle.

84 The Tsarevich Alexis Nicolaievich digging snow in the grounds of Tsarskoe Selo, 1913.

83

84

Austria-Hungary

During its last years the Austrian court gave off a dazzling brilliance, even though the Holy Roman Empire had been abolished in 1806 and what remained to the Habsburgs was reduced by the loss of their territories in Northern Italy and the Netherlands. But in 1867 the ancient dynasty could still claim rule over Austria, Hungary, and Bohemia, in addition to large areas of the Balkans. By the turn of the century the aged and much-loved Emperor Franz Josef had held the throne for as long as anyone could remember (since in fact the year of pan-European insurrection, 1848) and now reigned against the backdrop of Vienna at a moment of cultural climax. While Viennese society danced to Strauss, consumed rich pastries at Demel's, or attended the first performances of *The Merry Widow*, Freud and Jung were working on the revolutionary concept of

85 Empress Elisabeth of Austria, wife of Emperor Franz Josef I, in about the year 1870. Considered one of the most beautiful women in Europe, Elisabeth inherited to some degree the eccentricity of the Wittelsbachs of Bavaria, the family to which she belonged by birth. She loved to travel throughout Europe and built a house on the island of Corfu to which she could retreat to escape the demands of court life.

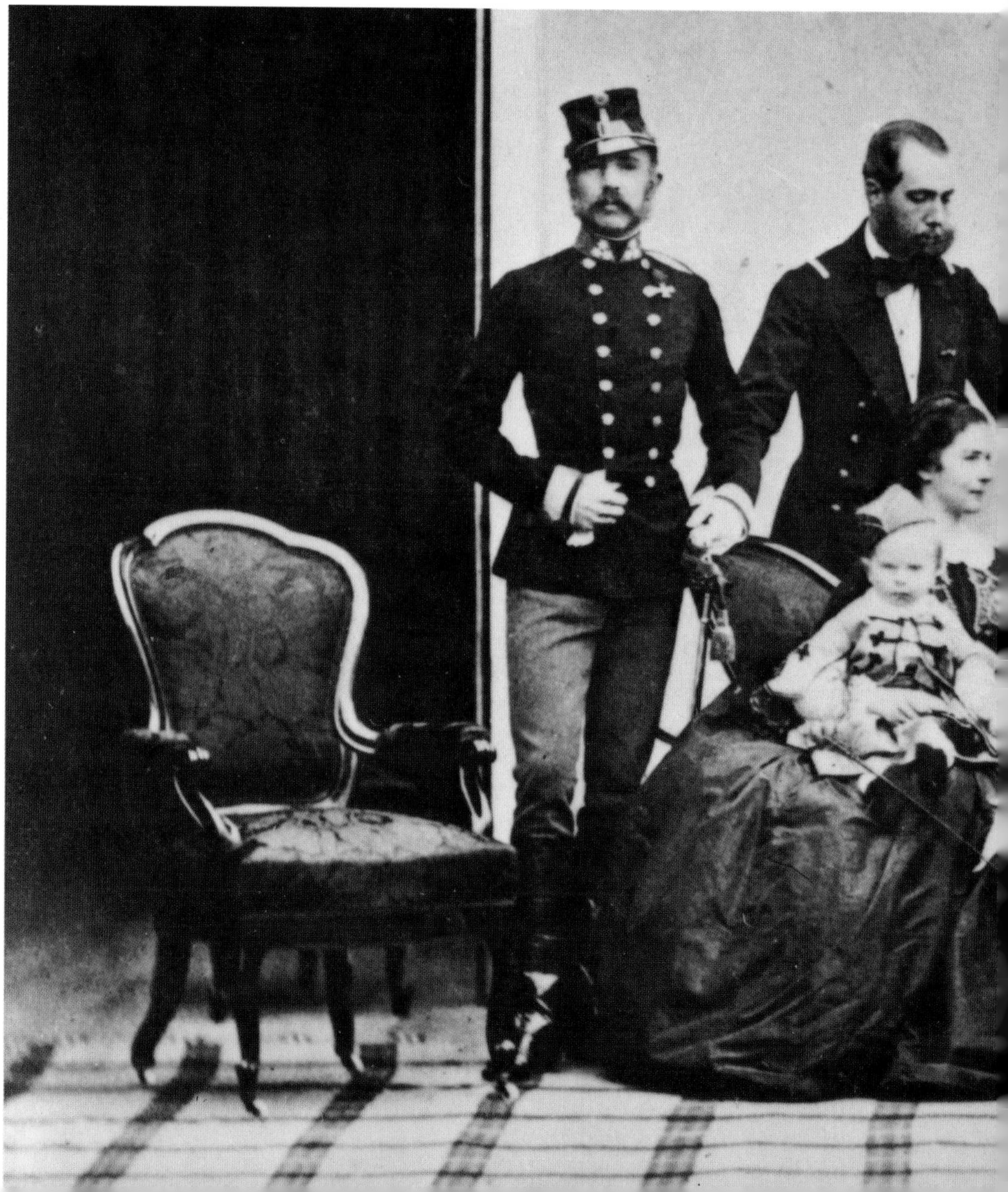

86 The Imperial family, 1860: back row, Emperor Franz Josef; his brother Maximilian and the latter's wife Charlotte (later Emperor and Empress of Mexico), Archduke Ludwig Victor and Archduke Karl Ludwig (also brothers). Front row: Empress Elisabeth holding her son Rudolf; her daughter Gisela; Archduchess Sophie and Archduke Franz Karl, the Emperor's parents.

87 *Overleaf* Empress Elisabeth on her deathbed, 10 September 1898. She was assassinated at Geneva while boarding a boat—stabbed in the chest, she nevertheless continued walking but collapsed some moments later.

psychiatry and Klimt, Schiele, and Otto Wagner were creating a new spirit in art and architecture.

Many of the great noble families of the Austro-Hungarian Empire maintained beautiful houses—or *palais*— in Vienna, usually named for their occupants. Among the finest were the Palais Esterhazy, the Palais Liechtenstein, and the Palais Kinsky. Owing to the illness and frequent absence of Empress Elisabeth, as well as to the dogged conservatism of the Emperor, it was the aristocracy, rather than the Imperial family, that provided Vienna with much of its glamour.

By 1914 the Habsburg clan had become enormously extended, making them the largest reigning family in Europe. Some thirty-one Archdukes and forty-four Archduchesses went about their obligations with, for the most part, a real sense of duty. They also seemed to enjoy their family life, thereby evincing a taste for domesticity passed down from the Empress Maria Theresia (r.1740–80).

In 1908 Vienna celebrated the Diamond Jubilee of Franz Josef, whose happiness had long since been shattered by a series of personal and dynastic tragedies: the assassination of the Emperor's brother Maximilian in 1867 by Mexican revolutionaries under Juárez; the dual suicide in 1889 of Crown Prince Rudolf and his young mistress; and the violent murder of Empress Elisabeth in 1898, the victim of an Italian anarchist in Geneva. The final blow would come in 1914, when the Emperor's nephew and heir, Archduke Franz Ferdinand, and his morganatic wife were assassinated at Sarajevo, the capital of the Balkan state of Bosnia.

86

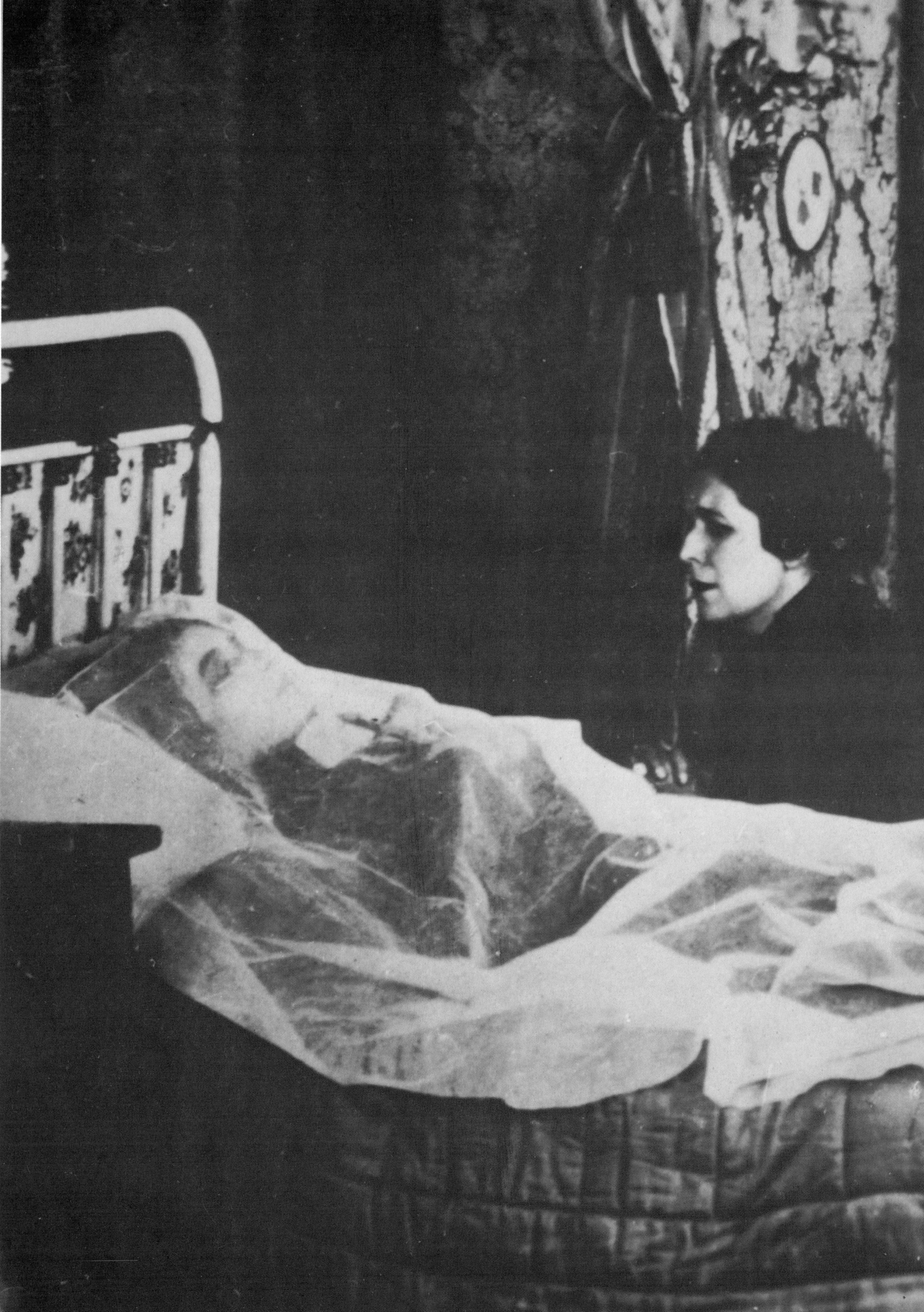

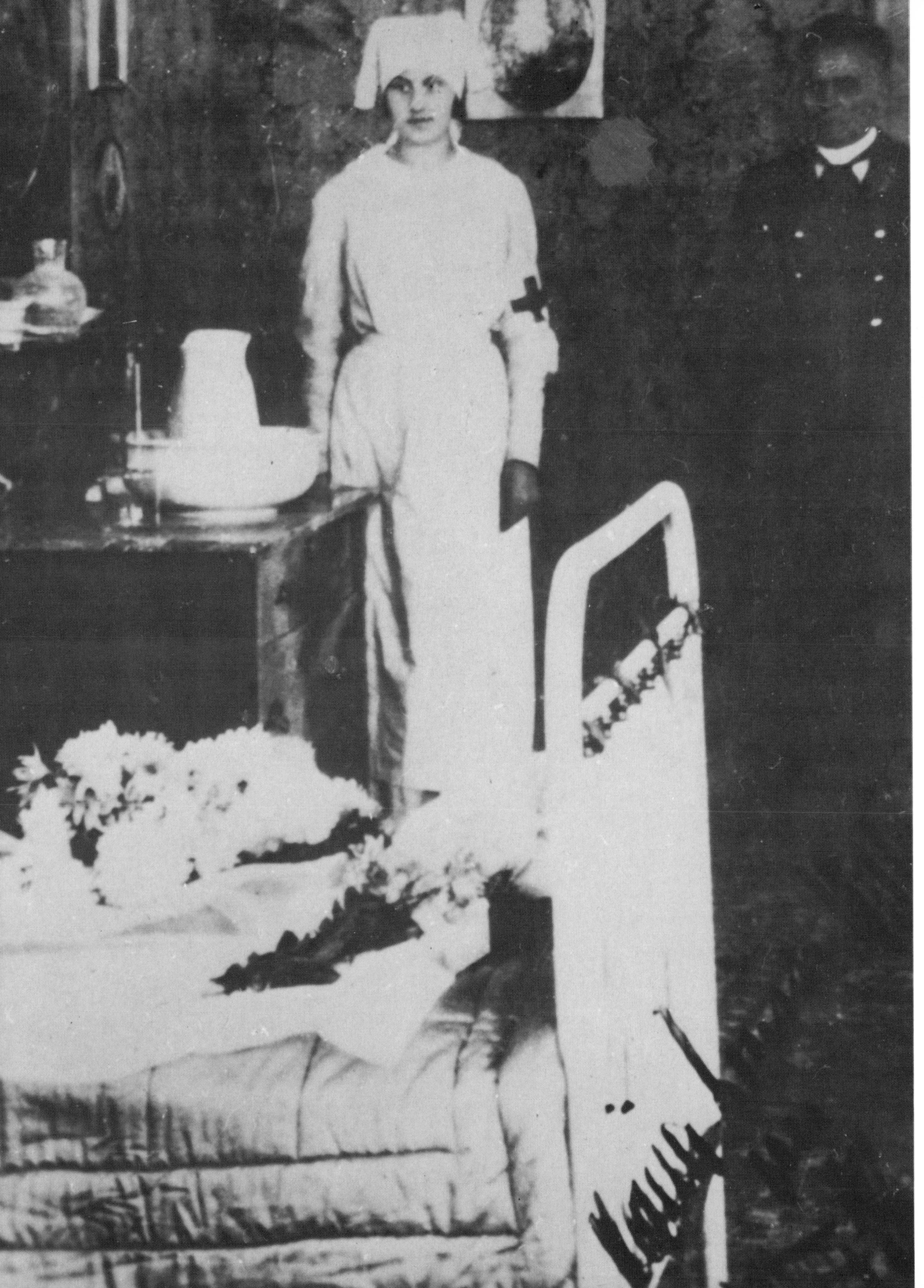

88

89

88 Archduchess Marie Valerie, the youngest child of the Emperor and Empress (born 1868), playing draughts with her mother's blackamoor. A gift from Khedive Ismail of Egypt, the boy was eventually allowed to return to his homeland.

89 Archduchess Marie Valerie with Countess Marie Larisch. The confidante of her aunt, the Empress, Countess Larisch was later excluded from the family circle after the death of Crown Prince Rudolf, because of her role as go-between for Rudolf and his mistress Marie Vetsera.

90 Archduchess Marie Valerie at her writing-desk. She was Elisabeth's favourite child.

The shots that rang out in Sarajevo plunged Europe into the abyss of World War I. In 1916, at the height of the conflict, Karl I, Franz Josef's great-nephew and the last of the Habsburg monarchs, mounted the Imperial throne. When the following year Karl and his wife Zita went to Budapest to be crowned King and Queen of Hungary, their coronation became the last thing of its kind on the European mainland, with the exception of the somewhat theatrical affair staged for King Ferdinand and Queen Marie of Roumania in 1922. Indeed, the Hungarian ceremony provided Europe with its last great royal occasion before the collapse of the three Continental empires. Although progressive in outlook, with much to offer postwar Austria, the monarchy of the last Habsburgs was swept away by the great wave of republican feeling that rolled over Europe in the aftermath of universal holocaust.

91 Archduchess Maria Theresia (right) playing a game with her children, Archduchesses Maria Annunciata and Elisabeth (front), and her stepchildren, Archduke Ferdinand Karl and Archduchess Margarete Sophie. Maria Theresia, an Infanta of Portugal (1855–1944), was the third wife of the Emperor's brother Archduke Karl Ludwig.

91

92

93

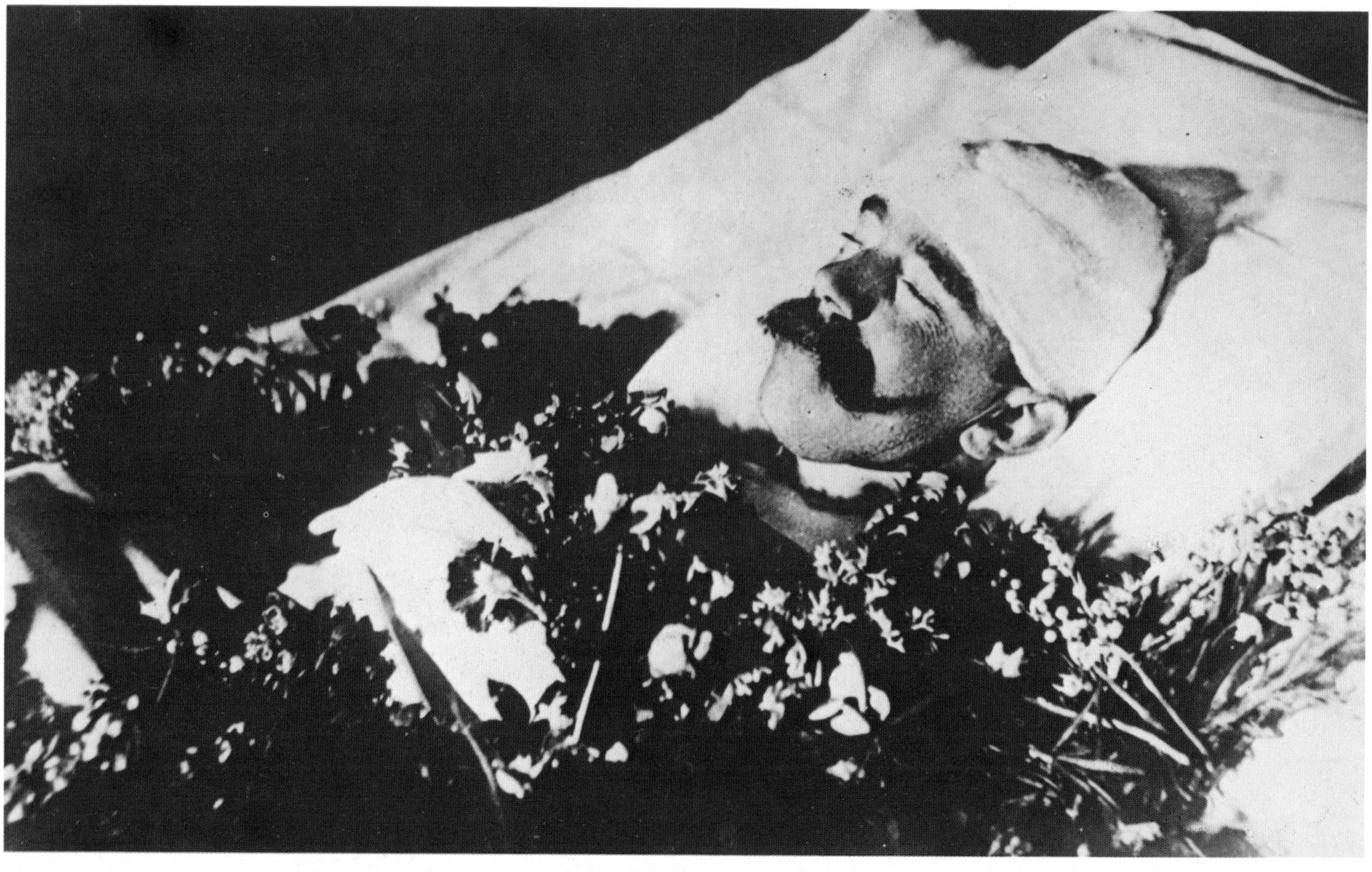

Pflanz · Linz ·

Erzh. Marie Valerie mit Jhren Kindern.

94

92 Crown Prince Rudolf, son and heir of the Emperor.

93 Rudolf on his deathbed. The exact circumstances of the tragedy at Mayerling have never been fully clarified and several conflicting theories have been put forward to explain the motives behind the double suicide of the Crown Prince and his mistress. A ballet and a film have been made on the subject.

94 Marie Valerie in 1900 with her children. From left to right, Archduchess Elisabeth Franziska, Archduke Franz Salvator, Archduchess Hedwig, Archduke Hubert Salvator, Archduke Theodor Salvator (dressed as a girl) and Archduchess Gertrud.

95 Archduchess Marie Valerie and her cousin, Archduke Franz Salvator, at the time of their engagement, 1890. She lived until 1924; her husband until 1939.

95

93

96 Emperor Franz Josef and members of the Imperial family at his Diamond Jubilee celebrations, outside the Schönbrunn Palace, Vienna, in 1908.

97 The Emperor at a mass at Innsbruck, August 1909, celebrating the centenary of a famous battle at which the Franco-Bavarian army was defeated.

98 Schoolchildren performing in the grounds of the Schönbrunn Palace before the Emperor, as part of the Diamond Jubilee celebrations.

99 Emperor Franz Josef walking behind the Blessed Sacrament in the annual Corpus Christi procession through the streets of Vienna, 1909.

102

100 Archduke Karl Ludwig, a younger brother of the Emperor, in his study. The father of Franz Ferdinand, he died in 1896.

101 Archduke Rainer and his first cousin, Archduchess Marie Karoline, on the occasion of their diamond wedding, February 1912. He died the following year; his wife, in 1915.

102 Emperor Franz Josef, in Tyrolean costume, coming down the steps of the Schönbrunn Palace, Vienna, to be greeted by a band of similarly attired *Waidmänner* (hunters), on the occasion of the fortieth anniversary of his accession, June 1898.

103 Archduke Wilhelm in fancy dress.

104 Archduchess Margarete Sophie (d. 1902) photographed in her robes as Abbess of the Theresan Convent of Noble Ladies of Prague. Situated in the Hradschin (Royal Palace) at Prague, the convent was an educational foundation open only to high-born young ladies, who before entering were obliged to prove that all sixteen of their great-great-grandparents were of noble birth. It was customary for the Abbess to be chosen from among the Archduchesses of the Imperial family. Both the Abbess and the pupils were free to leave the order and marry.

105 Emperor Franz Josef being greeted by the Chancellor, Prince Hohenlohe, on a visit to Bad Aussee.

104

105

106

106 Archduke Eugen in the robes of a Knight of the Order of St Stephen of Hungary.

107 Archduke Albrecht, of a younger branch of the family, in Tyrolean costume.

108 Archduchess Isabella, wife of Archduke Karl Ferdinand (nephew of Emperor Franz II), in full court dress, 1917.

107

109 Archduke Franz Salvator exchanging greetings with a loyal subject at the races.

110 The wedding of the future Emperor Karl and Empress Zita (right) at Schwarzau Castle, 1911. In the middle, standing to Emperor Franz Josef's right, is Archduchess Maria Josefa, daughter of King Georg I of Saxony and Karl's mother; the Duchess Maria Antonia of Parma, Zita's mother, is in profile at the left.

109

111 Franz Josef lying in state at the Schönbrunn Palace, 1916.

112 Archduke Franz Ferdinand and his morganatic wife Sophie, the Duchess of Hohenberg, at home in Vienna with their children, Duke Maximilian, Duke Ernst and Duchess Sophie. The children were barred from the succession, and when their parents were assassinated at Sarajevo their cousin Karl became the heir.

113 The Emperor on a country walk in 1913, at the age of eighty-three.

11

112

114 Archduke Karl and Archduchess Zita with their children, Archduchess Adelhaid and Archduke Otto (right).

115 Archduke Karl and Archduchess Zita being blessed by a rabbi on a visit to the Hungarian town of Pressburg.

115

CAFE THEE

Prussia

The elevation of Prussia from a minor German state to a great European power occurred mainly through the efforts of her Hohenzollern rulers, who in the seventeenth and eighteenth centuries learned to cultivate the military as a means of unifying a somewhat disparate collection of territories. Originally Electors of Brandenburg, the Hohenzollerns became Kings of Prussia in 1701, a century before any other German ruler assumed such a title. In the aftermath of the conquests carried out by Friedrich the Great (r. 1740–86), the abolition of the Holy Roman Empire in 1806 and the decline of Austria made it possible for Prussia to emerge as the most prominent state in Germany. A great leap forward came under Chancellor Otto von Bismarck who, following France's defeat in the Franco-Prussian War of 1870, realized the long-held Prussian ambition of welding the German states into one political entity. The vindictive Bismarck arranged for his monarch to be proclaimed Kaiser or Emperor on 18 January 1871, in the Hall of Mirrors at Versailles. The modest bearer of this arrogant crown, Wilhelm I, called the occasion 'the most dreadful day of my life'.

The entrenched militaristic traditions of Prussia had their effect on Imperial court life, imposing a highly regulated pattern of formal etiquette. Wilhelm's only son, Crown Prince Friedrich (Fritz), had married Queen Victoria's eldest daughter, the Princess Royal (Vicky), in 1858, and the latter's long correspondence with her mother reveals an English dislike of the rigours of the Prussian court. Two other English Princesses, Marie Louise and Alice, Countess of Athlone, would also sprinkle their accounts of Prussian court functions with complaints about the stifling atmosphere in which they unfolded.

Kaiser Wilhelm I, who as a young man had fought against Napoléon at the Battle of Leipzig, lived on until 1888, when finally he died just after his ninety-first birthday. Fritz succeeded him as Friedrich III, but cancer reduced his reign to little more than three months. Fritz and Vicky's twenty-six-year-old son succeeded to the throne as Wilhelm II. Fully embracing his role as heir to Prussian militarism, Wilhelm entertained Berlin with dress parades held at regular intervals, reviewed the troops from horseback, and lived to become 'the Kaiser' of World War I notoriety.

But for all its rather rigid formality, the Prussian court was not without its refinements, especially in the palaces built by the early rulers. The Castle and the Charlottenburg in Berlin and the Town Palace as well as Sans Souci at Potsdam must be counted among Europe's most splendid examples of eighteenth-century architecture, a period when, of course, the dominant influence came from the Bourbon court at Versailles.

In May 1913 Berlin witnessed its last great state occasion when the Emperor's only daughter, Princess Viktoria Luise, married Prince Ernst August of Hanover. It brought the final gathering of Europe's sovereigns before the outbreak of the Great War, among them King George V and Queen Mary as well as Emperor Nicholas II and Empress Alexandra, all of whom one year later would find themselves allied in war against their erstwhile host.

116 The lying-in-state of Wilhelm I, German Emperor and King of Prussia, March 1888. Wilhelm I succeeded his brother as King of Prussia in 1861, at the age of sixty-three; ten years later, after the Franco-Prussian War, he was proclaimed German Emperor at Versailles by Bismarck. He died at the age of ninety, having in his youth fought against Napoleon at the Battle of Leipzig.

118

117 The three eldest sons of Emperor Wilhelm II: Crown Prince Wilhelm, Prince Eitel Friedrich and Prince Adalbert, aged eleven, ten and nine respectively.

118 Prince Oskar, fifth son of the Emperor, in military uniform.

119 Emperor Wilhelm II—'Kaiser Bill'—on the terrace of the Villa Achilleon, his house at Corfu, formerly the property of Empress Elisabeth of Austria.

119

120

121

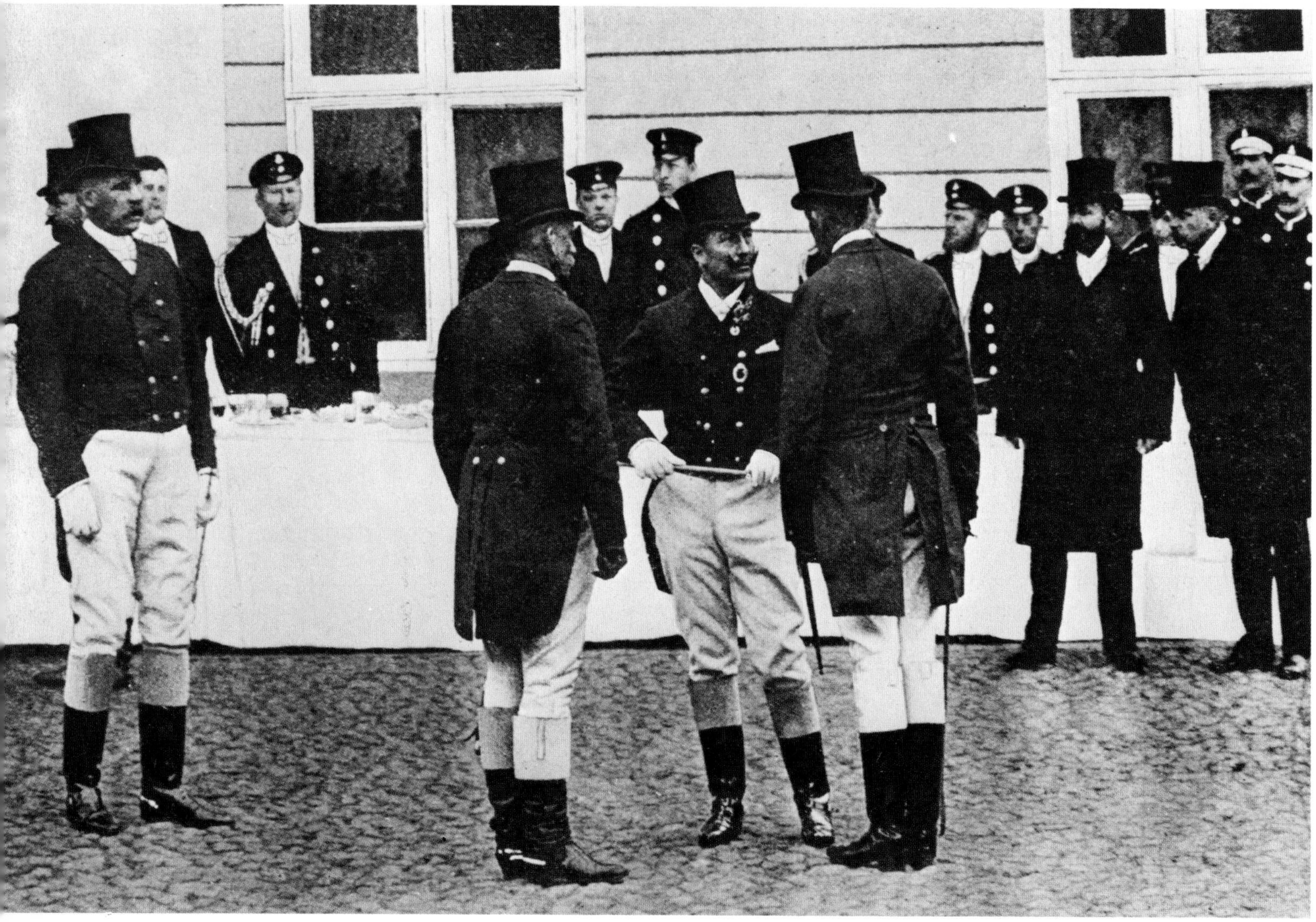

120 Wilhelm II and his courtiers in the costume of Frederick the Great's time; the Emperor is dressed as Frederick himself and his hand rests on the shoulder of the painter Adolf Menzel. To the left is Count Eulenburg.

121 Wilhelm II in riding habit.

122 The Empress Friedrich receiving a presentation from a pupil at the Augusta School, Friedenshof, in 1900, the year before her death.

122

123 The Empress Friedrich and her family in 1897 at Castle Friedrichshof, which she had had built in the Taunus mountains. The eldest daughter of Queen Victoria, 'Vicky' was married to the future Emperor Friedrich III in 1858, and was the mother of the last German Emperor, Wilhelm II. From left to right are three of her sons-in-law—Crown Prince Constantine of Greece (later King Constantine I), Prince Adolf of Schaumburg-Lippe, Viktoria's husband (behind), Prince Friedrich Karl of Hesse; the Empress Friedrich, her fourth daughter Princess Margarete of Prussia, her nephew Prince Albert of Schleswig-Holstein, her third daughter Crown Princess Sophie of Greece (later Queen Sophie) and her second daughter Princess Viktoria of Prussia. Foreground, from left to right, Vicky's grandchildren: Prince Maximilian of Hesse, Prince Friedrich Wilhelm of Hesse, Prince George of Greece (later King George II), Prince Alexander of Greece (later King Alexander I) and Princess Helen of Greece (later Queen of Roumania).

124

125

126

127

124 Empress Auguste Viktoria, wife of Emperor Wilhelm II, on a visit to the German orphanage in London, 1911.

125 Prince Heinrich of Prussia, younger brother of Emperor Wilhelm II, with King Chulalongkorn of Siam, during a visit to Bangkok. Between the Prince and the King is Crown Prince Vajirunhis of Siam, who died in 1895; the second row consists entirely of brothers of King Chulalongkorn.

126 Princess Charlotte of Prussia, eldest sister of Emperor Wilhelm II, and first granddaughter of Queen Victoria (she was born in 1860). Princess Charlotte was married to Duke Bernhard III of Saxe-Meiningen, and died in 1919.

127 Empress Auguste Viktoria admiring a portrait of her husband, Emperor Wilhelm II.

128 Crown Prince Wilhelm and his fiancée, Duchess Cecilie of Mecklenburg-Schwerin, receiving bouquets from schoolchildren at Castle Gelbensande at the time of their engagement, September 1904.

129 Crown Prince Wilhelm and Crown Princess Cecilie entering a coach on the christening day of their first child, Wilhelm, at Potsdam, July 1906.

130 *Overleaf* Since the days of Frederick the Great the Prussian court had delighted in military reviews. In this picture his great-great-great-great-nephew, Wilhelm II, takes the salute at a parade in Berlin. This photograph formed part of an album of the event which the Emperor sent to his uncle King Edward VII.

129

131 The Emperor among his cavalry troops.

132 Emperor Wilhelm II installing his fifth son, Prince Oskar, in the First Regiment of Foot Guards at Potsdam. To the right are the Emperor's four eldest sons, Crown Prince Wilhelm, Prince Eitel Friedrich, Prince Adalbert and Prince August Wilhelm, all wearing this regiment's uniform with its curious tall helmets.

131

132

133 Princess Viktoria Luise (left), only daughter of Emperor Wilhelm II, in her uniform of the Death's Head Hussars, and her sister-in-law, Princess Sophie Charlotte (the wife of Prince Eitel Friedrich), as Colonel of Dragoons, at a military review, 1911. The custom of royal ladies being given military rank and attending parades riding side-saddle originated in Germany and later became the fashion throughout Europe. Princess Viktoria Luise died in 1980 at the age of 88. She was the mother of Queen Frederika of Greece and the grandmother of King Constantine of Greece and Queen Sofia of Spain.

133

134 Emperor Wilhelm II, Empress Auguste Viktoria and King Edward VII (back to camera) at a garden party at Wilhelmshöhe, 1907.

135 Emperor Wilhelm II with his uncle, King Edward VII (wearing German uniform), at Wilhelmshöhe in 1900.

136 The Emperor inspecting soldiers on parade at Potsdam, 1912.

136

137 Empress Auguste Viktoria with, from left to right, Prince Hubertus, her only daughter Princess Viktoria Luise, Prince Wilhelm, Prince Louis Ferdinand and her daughter-in-law Crown Princess Cecilie, at the annual Stiftungsfest (Foundation Day) at Potsdam.

138 Crown Princess Cecilie in period costume, 1913.

139 Crown Prince Wilhelm (standing, centre), Crown Princess Cecilie (right), Fräulein von Trotha (centre) and Countess Pourtalis (left) tobogganing at St Moritz, 1907.

138

139

140

140 Crown Princess Cecilie visiting a girls' school in Berlin, 1913.

141 The Emperor at sea.

142 Emperor Wilhelm II and King Friedrich August III of Saxony at the unveiling of a statue to commemorate the centenary of the Battle of Leipzig, 1913.

143 Prince Wilhelm, eldest son of Crown Prince Wilhelm, on a rocking horse, bearing the Hohenzollern standard. This idealized portrait, taken in 1907, was entitled 'Der jüngste Kavallerist'—the youngest cavalier.

141

143

142

even Detmold, the capital of the tiny principality of Lippe, had its opera house—and a fine one at that.

Of all the German courts, the richest in ceremonial and pageantry was that of the Wittelsbachs. Munich, with its glittering palaces and churches, formed a superb setting for royal occasions, and the annual procession of the robed Knights of Saint George, from the Residenz to the Theatinerkirche, gave Europe one of its truly dazzling sights.

Within days after the end of the Great War and the abdication of Emperor Wilhelm II in November 1918, all twenty of the German monarchies were abolished, bringing down the centuries-old kingdoms, grand duchies, duchies, and principalities like a great house of playing-cards.

145

145 Prince Regent Luitpold of Bavaria photographed on the occasion of his ninetieth birthday, 1911.

146 Prince Ludwig Ferdinand of Bavaria in his Munich clinic, 1914. The Prince was a practising doctor of medicine.

146

147 King Ludwig III and Queen Maria Theresia of Bavaria riding through the streets of Würzburg during a centenary celebration, 1914. Maria Theresia was also the Jacobite claimant to the British throne, and as such was regarded by the few remaining legitimists as 'Queen Mary III'.

148 Duchess Maria Josefa of Bavaria (née Infanta of Portugal), wife of Duke Karl Theodor, in 1909. She was the mother of Queen Elisabeth of the Belgians, wife of Albert I. The ducal title in Bavaria was borne by members of the junior branch of the Royal Family.

148

149 King Ludwig III of Bavaria in the last procession of the Knights of the Order of St George, which took place in 1913. In the lion helmet is Count Felix von Bothmer, captain of the bodyguards.

150 The lying-in-state of Prince Regent Luitpold of Bavaria in the Hofkirche, Munich, December 1912. He was Regent for the last twenty-six years of his life, during the insanity of Otto I.

151 *Overleaf left* Crown Princess Marie Gabriele of Bavaria with her eldest son, Prince Luitpold, in 1912. She was to die that same year; her son, two years later. She was the daughter of Duke Karl Theodor.

152 *Overleaf right* Prince Rudolf of Bavaria, third son of Crown Prince Rupprecht, in 1910. He died in 1912 at the age of three. The *art nouveau* vase beside which he is photographed is a typical product of the Secession style, for which Munich became famous in the early years of this century.

149

Luitpold Prinz von Bayern
des Königr. Bayern Verweser
geb. 12. März 1821, gest. 12. Dez.
RUPPRECH

153 King Ludwig III and Queen Maria Theresia in the throne-room of the Residenz, Munich, on their installation as the last monarchs of Bavaria, 12 November 1913. There was particular rejoicing on this occasion, as Otto I had been King in name only for so long. A year after Ludwig became Regent the Landtag decided to proclaim him King, although Otto was still alive in his castle of Fürstenried.

154 King Otto I of Bavaria on his deathbed. He succeeded to the throne on the death of his elder brother, King Ludwig II, in 1886. He was mentally deranged throughout his reign of twenty-seven years and was finally deposed in 1913 by the then Prince Regent. King Otto died in 1916. Apart from photographs of him as a boy this is the only known picture of him.

154

155

156

155 Grand Duke Friedrich I and Grand Duchess Luise of Baden on the occasion of his Golden Jubilee, 1906.

156 Dowager Grand Duchess Luise of Baden with her daughter, Queen Victoria of Sweden, and her great-grandson, Prince Lennart of Sweden, 1914. Dowager Grand Duchess Luise was the only daughter of Wilhelm I, German Emperor and King of Prussia.

157 Grand Duchess Luise of Baden with her daughter, Crown Princess (later Queen) Victoria of Sweden, 1907. Both are wearing two tiaras.

158 The Princely Family of Waldeck and Pyrmont in the drawing-room of Castle Arolsen, 1877. From left to right, Princess Pauline, a lady-in-waiting, Princess Emma (later Queen of the Netherlands and mother of Queen Wilhelmina), Prince Georg Viktor, Hereditary Prince Friedrich, Princess Helena, Princess Elisabeth and Princess Helena the younger (later Duchess of Albany and mother of Princess Alice, Countess of Athlone). The rest of the group is unidentified.

157

158

159

Marie Elly Aunt Augusta at 90. Adolphu

159 Dowager Grand Duchess Augusta of Mecklenburg-Strelitz, aged ninety, greeting her niece, Queen Mary, at Neustrelitz in 1912. Standing with back to the camera is Grand Duke Adolf Friedrich V; to the left of the photograph is Grand Duchess Elisabeth, with her daughter, Duchess Marie, and to the right are Princess Mary (later the Princess Royal) and Hereditary Grand Duke Adolf Friedrich. Dowager Grand Duchess Augusta was the daughter of Prince Adolphus, Duke of Cambridge, seventh son of King George III. She died in 1914 at the age of ninety-two.

160 Duke Johann Albrecht and Duchess Elisabeth of Mecklenburg-Schwerin being greeted by young ladies during their visit to Brunswick, following the Duke's appointment as Regent of the Duchy in 1907.

160

161 Princess Feodora Reuss (Younger Line), Grand Duchess Eleonore of Hesse and by Rhine and Duke Johann Albrecht of Mecklenburg-Schwerin at a fancy-dress ball given by the latter on becoming Regent of the Duchy of Brunswick, 1907.

162 Duchess Altburg and Duchess Ingeborg Alix, daughters of Grand Duke Friedrich August of Oldenburg.

163 Prince Adolf of Schaumburg-Lippe (second from right), his wife, Princess Viktoria (third from right) and Princess Marie Anna of Schaumburg-Lippe (next to Viktoria) on the beach of a north German seaside resort, 1913. Princess Viktoria was a younger sister of Emperor Wilhelm II.

162

163

164 Princess Marie of Saxe-Coburg-Gotha, daughter of the Duke of Edinburgh, on the day of her marriage to Crown Prince Ferdinand of Roumania at Castle Sigmaringen, 10 January 1893.

165 The wedding of Princess Alexandra of Saxe-Coburg-Gotha and Prince Ernst of Hohenlohe-Langenburg at Coburg, 20 April 1896. From left to right are Grand Duke Ernst and Grand Duchess Victoria Melita of Hesse and by Rhine, Crown Princess Marie of Roumania, Prince Alfred Duke of Edinburgh and Saxe-Coburg-Gotha, Wilhelm II, German Emperor and King of Prussia, Grand Duchess Marie Pavlovna (the elder) of Russia, Princess Marie Duchess of Edinburgh and Saxe-Coburg-Gotha, the Duchess of York (the future Queen Mary), Auguste Viktoria, German Empress and Queen of Prussia, Princess Elise Reuss, Princess Beatrice of Saxe-Coburg-Gotha, Princess Louise of Saxe-Coburg-Gotha (daughter of King Leopold II of the Belgians and wife of Prince Philip), Princess Feodora of Saxe-Meiningen, the Duke of York (the future King George V), Crown Prince Ferdinand of Roumania, Prince Heinrich XXVII Reuss, Prince Alfred of Saxe-Coburg-Gotha, Prince Max of Baden, Count Albert von Mensdorff-Pouilly and Prince Philip of Saxe-Coburg-Gotha.

164

165

166 Grand Duke Wilhelm Ernst and Grand Duchess Caroline of Saxe-Weimar-Eisenach riding in procession through the streets of Weimar, 1903.

167 The Princely Family of Reuss at the wedding of King Ferdinand of Bulgaria and Princess Eleonore Reuss (Younger Line)—Castle Osterstein, Gera, 1 March 1908. Seated beside the bride (who is third from the right in the second row) is Grand Duchess Marie Pavlovna (the elder) of Russia, who 'arranged' the marriage. It was the custom in Reuss, the bride's homeland, to name all male members of the Princely Family Heinrich in honour of the Holy Roman Emperor, Heinrich VI, from whom they had received their lands in the thirteenth century. A complicated system of numbering was developed, which by the nineteenth century took two different forms: the Elder Line completed a sequence of one to a hundred, before returning to one; the Younger Line numbered the first Heinrich to be born in each century as number one, and followed the sequence through till the end of

the century. The highest numeral reached was at the end of the eighteenth century with Prince Heinrich LXXVIII. Although the Elder Line became extinct some years ago the Younger Line still follows this curious custom.

168 King Friedrich August III of Saxony and his sons on the beach at the north German island of Juist, 1912. In the background is the Kurhaus.

169 King Friedrich August III of Saxony (centre, top table) taking beer with the students at Heidelberg University, 1914.

170 *Overleaf* The crowd in front of the Ducal Palace at Brunswick acclaiming the new Duke and Duchess, 1913. The monarchy was re-established at that date by Emperor Wilhelm II on the occasion of his daughter Viktoria Luise's marriage to Prince Ernst August of Hanover, heir to the Duchy of Brunswick.

168

169

Belgium, Luxembourg and The Netherlands

171 King Léopold I of the Belgians, who was elected King of the newly independent country in 1830. Formerly Prince Leopold of Saxe-Saalfeld-Coburg, he was uncle to both Queen Victoria and Prince Albert.

Their countries having gained independence only in the nineteenth century, the courts of Belgium, Luxembourg and The Netherlands are relatively young. More important, they all continue to flourish.

The oldest is the Dutch house of Orange, whose princes had been hereditary *Stadhouders* until after the Napoleonic wars, when they became first Sovereign Princes and then Kings. The royal dynasty began with King Willem I (formerly Prince Willem VI of Orange), who was installed at Amsterdam in 1814. He also reigned as Grand Duke of Luxembourg.

Modern Belgium came into being in 1830 after King Willem's southern provinces rebelled, broke away, and found a monarch of their own in the person of Prince Leopold of Saxe-Coburg-Gotha, uncle to both Queen Victoria and Prince Albert. But the house of Orange, despite this loss, grew in popularity among the Dutch along with the increasing prosperity of nineteenth-century Holland, whose great wealth was derived to a considerable extent from trade with the Dutch East Indies.

Willem II succeeded his father in 1840 and reigned until 1849, which brought the accession of his own son, Willem III. But when the last of this King's surviving sons, the Prince of Orange, died (after each of the monarch's brothers had also died), a dynastic crisis arose, prompting the elderly Willem to look around Europe for a new bride. Thus, in 1897, the sixty-one-year-old sovereign married twenty-year-old Princess Emma, daughter of the reigning Prince of Waldeck and Pyrmont. A year later the issue of this union was a daughter, Wilhelmina. But with the death of King Willem in 1890, Wilhelmina could inherit only the crown of Holland, since Salic law forbade the succession of a woman in Luxembourg. As a consequence, Luxembourg separated from the Netherlands and a second court was established under Duke Adolphe of Nassau, a distant kinsman of the ten-year-old Queen Wilhelmina.

During the minority of the Dutch Queen, her mother served as Regent. Meanwhile, the young girl paid a visit to Queen Victoria at Windsor Castle, where the English sovereign, now quite elderly, is reputed to have said to her: 'As we're two Queens together, we can say what we like!'

Queen Wilhelmina was installed at the age of eighteen in a magnificent ceremony at Amsterdam's Nieuwe Kerk. Wearing a heavy ermine-lined velvet mantle, she walked in procession from the royal palace to the church accompanied by Queen Emma.

Appropriately enough in a nation devoted to solid bourgeois values, the Dutch court had never attempted the splendour characteristic of princely life elsewhere. Now simplicity came quite naturally, since the royal family consisted only of Queen Wilhelmina and Dowager Queen Emma until 1901, when the reigning monarch married Duke Heinrich of Mecklenburg-Schwerin. Then with the birth of Princess Juliana in 1909 the dynasty gained an heir, to the great joy of the Dutch people, who had feared their royal house was once again in danger of becoming extinct.

The Belgian court at Brussels, which came into being under King Leopold I and

176
Parl
acce

172 King Léopold II of the Belgians on a visit to the Riviera.

173 Queen Marie-Henriette of the Belgians, wife of King Léopold II, at the races in a bath-chair, 1902. This was her last outing.

173

182 Princess Marie-Adélaïde, later Grand Duchess of Luxembourg, who succeeded her father Guillaume IV in 1912.

183 Queen Emma of the Netherlands in 1883. She was the second wife of King Willem III, and became Regent for her daughter Wilhelmina in 1890.

184 Queen Wilhelmina of the Netherlands seated with her mother Queen Emma at her installation in the Nieuwe Kerk, Amsterdam, on 6 September 1898.

183

184

185

185 Queen Wilhelmina and Prince Hendrik with Princess Juliana on the balcony of the Royal Palace in Amsterdam, 1909.

186 Crowds of children waving streamers outside the Royal Palace, Amsterdam, following the birth of Princess Juliana in 1909. The birth of the princess was hailed as a great national occasion. At the time the Royal Family consisted only of her mother Queen Wilhelmina, her father Prince Hendrik (formerly Duke Heinrich of Mecklenburg-Schwerin) and her grandmother Queen Emma, and the House of Orange was in danger of becoming extinct.

187 Queen Wilhelmina at a military review.

187

186

188 Queen Wilhelmina, Prince Hendrik and Princess Juliana in seventeenth-century Dutch costume. The Queen and her family were at the time posing for a painting, and they do indeed look exactly like figures from a seventeenth-century *genre* scene.

188

189

189 Queen Wilhelmina leaving the Dutch Parliament after the State Opening in 1918. The state coach was made specially for her, and its panels are painted with scenes showing the prosperous Dutch overseas empire.

190 The Queen and her husband and daughter with the officers and crew of a Dutch battleship.

190

191

191 Queen Wilhelmina (right) and a lady-in-waiting teaching Princess Juliana to skate, 1917.

192 The Royal Barge of the Netherlands.

193 Queen Wilhelmina waiting to greet the French President, arriving on the Royal Barge during his state visit in 1911.

192

19

France

Post-revolutionary France experimented with several different forms of government, at various times calling herself an empire, a kingdom, and a republic. But one way or another, Paris had an official court life, with only occasional interruptions, from the beginning of the nineteenth century until 1870, when the Franco-Prussian War sent Napoléon III and Empress Eugénie into exile. The first Empire, of course, had been that of Napoléon I (r. 1804–15), whose Empresses were first Joséphine de Beauharnais (1804–9) and then Marie-Louise of Austria (1810–15). After the fall of Napoléon, the original Bourbon line returned to power under Louis XVI's two brothers, Louis XVIII (r. 1815–24) and Charles X (r. 1824–30), whose attempts to roll back the Revolution cost their dynasty the throne of France forever. When Charles X abdicated in 1830 he was succeeded by the 'July Monarch' or 'Citizen King' Louis-Philippe, a descendant of the Orléans branch of the Bourbon family, which originated—in the seventeenth century—with 'Monsieur', the brother of Louis XIV. Styling himself 'King of the French', Louis-Philippe assumed the role of *bon bourgeois* and played the stock market, exhorting his subjects: '*Enrichissez-vous*!' Needless to say, this was a reign more stodgy than glittering, and the bored French rebelled again in 1848, the year that set so many crowns askew. As Louis-Philippe and Queen Marie-Amélie sought refuge abroad, the monarchy was again abolished in favour of a republic.

But when the French elected their new President, he was none other than Prince Louis-Napoléon, the son of Napoléon I's brother, who had been made King of Holland, and the daughter of Empress Joséphine by her first marriage. Four years later a *coup d'état* made him Emperor of the French, and with the beautiful and vivacious Eugénie de Montijo as his Empress, Napoléon III initiated what would be the last French court.

Like all their predecessors since the Revolution, Napoléon III and Eugénie established their court at the Tuileries Palace, a vast addition to the Louvre complex begun by Queen Marie de'Medici in the mid-sixteenth century. Although not living at Versailles, the Imperial couple did everything to rival the brilliance of life under the *ancien régime*. With Eugénie consciously emulating the dress and style of Marie-Antoinette, the whole era assumed the character of *opéra bouffe*, the very sort of *boulevard* entertainment that Offenbach was then bringing to glorious climax. To make Paris a suitable setting for the new Imperial era, Napoléon commissioned Baron Haussmann to rebuild the capital with all the opulent classicism that we know today. In this *ville lumière*, state occasions were numerous, and they have rarely seemed more colourful or grand, especially when they involved official visits from various European sovereigns. The culminating event was probably the Universal Exhibition of 1867, whose opening ceremony was attended by Emperor Alexander II of Russia, Emperor Franz Josef of

194 The Imperial Court at Fontainebleau, 1860. In the foreground, in the boat, are Emperor Napoléon III and the Prince Imperial. Empress Eugénie is seated third from the left, with her hand raised. Prince Metternich is at the extreme right, in a top hat.

Austria, the Prince of Wales, Sultan Abdul Aziz of Turkey, and Khedive Ismail of Egypt.

The Franco-Prussian War and the ensuing Commune brought down the Second Empire; but still, centuries of monarchical rule had given Paris a royal look that no amount of republicanism could take away. By now a city of irresistible charm and beauty, it attracted crowned heads from all over the world, many of whom made the city their second home, especially the exiles, such as Grand Dukes Alexis Alexandrovich and Paul Alexandrovich, both banished because of their marriages, and Queen Isabella II of Spain.

Although the former Emperor and his Bourbon counterpart were after 1871 forbidden by law from entering the capital, other members of the Imperial and Royal families could move about as they pleased. Meanwhile, France's Third Republic welcomed state visits from Tsar Nicholas II, King Alfonso XIII of Spain, and Queen Wilhelmina of The Netherlands. Indeed, a royal subculture grew up in republican Paris and did much to give the *belle époque* its special flavour of febrile, exotic splendour. And nowhere is nostalgia for the royal past more indulged than in late twentieth-century Paris.

196

195

198

195 Napoléon III with his son, the Prince Imperial.

196 'Plon-Plon', Prince Napoléon, son of Napoléon I's brother Jérôme, King of Westphalia, and of Princess Clotilde of Savoy, daughter of King Vittorio Emanuele II,with his sons, Prince Victor and Prince Louis, photographed by Nadar.

197 Empress Eugénie posing as an odalisque during a visit to Egypt, 1869.

198 Empress Eugénie on a visit to Algeria, 1869.

197

199

200

199 The last Bourbon Queen, Marie-Amélie, wife of King Louis-Philippe of the French, in old age. She died in exile in England in 1866.

200 Emperor Napoléon III and Empress Eugénie.

201 The coffin of Queen Isabella II of Spain lying in state at a Paris railway station before being transported to Spain for burial. Queen Isabella, who was deposed in 1868, went into exile in Paris, where she died on 9 April 1904.

202 *Overleaf* The funeral procession of Grand Duke Alexis Alexandrovich of Russia (b. 1850), brother of Emperor Alexander III, passing through the streets of Paris, 18 November 1908.

SCALA SCALA

203 Prince George of Greece and his fiancée, Princess Marie Bonaparte, on their engagement, 1907. Daughter of the distinguished geographer and botanist, Prince Roland Bonaparte, Princess Marie was the author of several works on psychoanalysis, and was instrumental in aiding Sigmund Freud's departure from Vienna during the 1930s. Her maternal grandfather, François Blanc, was responsible for the building of the Casino at Monte Carlo.

205 Prince Ferdinand of Orléans, Duke of Montpensier (standing, right) giving a talk on his explorations of the temples of Angkor, Paris, 1910. Seated in the front row, from left to right, are Mme Perez Caballero, Grand Duchess Marie Pavlovna (the elder) of Russia, Princess Henriette of Orléans, Duchess of Vendôme, and Prince Gaston of Orléans, Count d'Eu. In the second row, left to right, the Duchess de Noailles, Countess d'Haussonville, the Duchess d'Uzès, the Duke of Vendôme, Prince Roland Bonaparte and M. Perez Caballero. It is interesting to note the presence of a member of the House of Bonaparte at a lecture given by a member of the House of Bourbon.

204 The christening of Prince Pedro Henrique of Orléans and Braganza, grandson of Crown Princess Isabel, at the Château d'Eu, September 1909. From left to right, Baroness St Joaquim, Abbé Gérard, Prince Louis of Orléans and Braganza and Crown Princess Isabel of Brazil, Countess d'Eu. The christening was performed with water brought from the source of the Carioca. After the abolition of the Brazilian monarchy in 1889 Crown Princess Isabel went into exile in France, the country of birth of her husband, Prince Gaston of Orléans, Count d'Eu, grandson of King Louis-Philippe of the French.

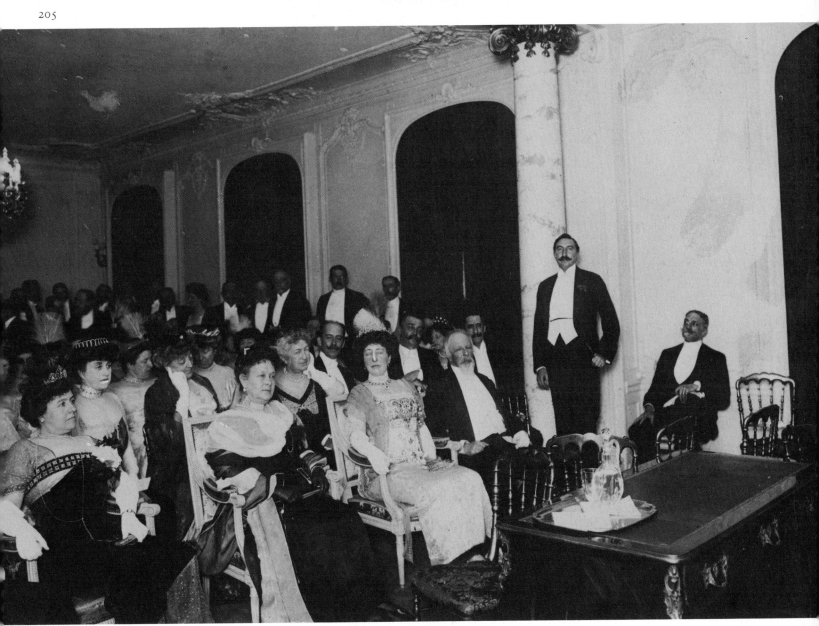

204

205

206 Prince Ferdinand of Orléans, Duke of Montpensier (1884–1924), the distinguished traveller and explorer, on a trip to Africa, circa 1909.

207 A group of mourners leaving the station at Dreux, Normandy, for the funeral of Prince Robert of Orléans, Duke of Chartres, December 1910.

206

207

208

208 The Countess of Paris and her son, Prince Ferdinand of Orléans, Duke of Montpensier, on board the Prince's yacht *Mekong*, 1913.

209 Queen Wilhelmina of the Netherlands protecting her ears during the firing of a cannon on her visit to Paris, June 1912.

209

210 King George V and President Poincaré at the Hôtel de Ville, Paris, April 1914, during the King's state visit to France.

211 Infanta Eulalia of Spain (left) and the Countess of Hohenfelsen (later Princess Paley, morganatic wife of Grand Duke Michael Mihailovich of Russia) at a fancy-dress party given in Paris by Countess d'Yturbe, 1912.

212 Empress Eugénie in exile in 1914, at the age of eighty-eight. The Empress accompanied her husband, Emperor Napoléon III, into exile in England in 1870 and lived at Farnborough. She died fifty years later, in 1920, at the age of ninety-four.

211

214 King Oscar II of Sweden in state robes.

215 Queen Lovisa of Sweden, wife of King Karl XV, in state robes.

216 The coronation of Oscar II of Sweden as King of Norway at Trondheim Cathedral, 18 July 1873. Until 1905 the Kingdoms of Norway and Sweden were united under one monarch. The coronation of King Oscar was the last of a Swedish King in Norway, as well as being the first ever European coronation to be photographed.

214

215

216

217 The state opening of the Swedish Parliament by King Oscar II, 1904. Seated, from left to right, are Prince Wilhelm Duke of Södermanland, Crown Prince Gustaf (later King Gustaf V), King Oscar, Prince Gustaf Adolf (later King Gustaf VI Adolf) and Prince Carl Duke of Västergötland. Not only the King, but also all the royal Princes are wearing crowns and state robes, a practice which ceased after 1907.

married Princess Maud, the daughter of Edward VII and Queen Alexandra. Together the young couple were crowned at Trondheim Cathedral in 1906. The beginning of a fifty-one-year reign, the ceremony was the last of its kind in Scandinavia, where all three monarchies abandoned traditional pomp in favour of a mere oath of office taken to mark the formal accession of a new sovereign. This simplification of formalities may help to account for the fact that the three lesser houses of Europe's extreme north still hold their thrones today.

217

N
A

218 The arrival of Emperor Nicholas II and Empress Alexandra Feodorovna of Russia at Stockholm on the occasion of their state visit to Sweden.

219 The Swedish Royal Barge bringing back Prince Gustaf Adolf (later King Gustaf VI Adolf) and his bride Princess Margaretha from their honeymoon in Ireland, 9 July 1905. Princess Margaretha, formerly Princess Margaret of Connaught, was the elder daughter of Prince Arthur, Duke of Connaught, and a granddaughter of Queen Victoria. After their marriage at St George's Chapel, Windsor Castle, the young Prince took his bride back to Sweden to live in the castle of Rosendal.

219

220 The lying-in-state of King Oscar II, December 1907.

221 The christening of Prince Sigvard, Duke of Upland, June 1907. Seated, left to right, Princess Therese Duchess of Dalecarlia, King Oscar, Princess Margaretha with Prince Sigvard, Queen Sophia and Princess Ingeborg Duchess of Västergötland with Princess Astrid (later Queen Astrid of the Belgians). Standing, Prince Eugen Duke of Nerike, Prince Wilhelm Duke of Södermanland, Crown Prince Gustaf (later King Gustaf V), Prince Gustaf Adolf (later King Gustaf VI Adolf) with Prince Gustaf Adolf, and Prince Carl Duke of Västergötland. Seated in foreground, Princess Margaretha (later Princess Axel of Denmark) and Princess Märtha (later Crown Princess Märtha of Norway).

220

221

222 Prince Wilhelm of Sweden, Duke of Södermanland (left) and his elder brother Prince Gustaf Adolf (later King Gustaf VI Adolf), sons of Crown Prince Gustaf (later King Gustaf V) and Crown Princess Victoria.

223 Crown Princess Margaretha (formerly Princess Margaret of Connaught), with her third son, Prince Bertil, 1913. After her death in 1920, Crown Prince Gustaf Adolf married another English bride, Lady Louise Mountbatten (elder sister of the late Lord Mountbatten of Burma), who later became Queen Louise of Sweden.

222

223

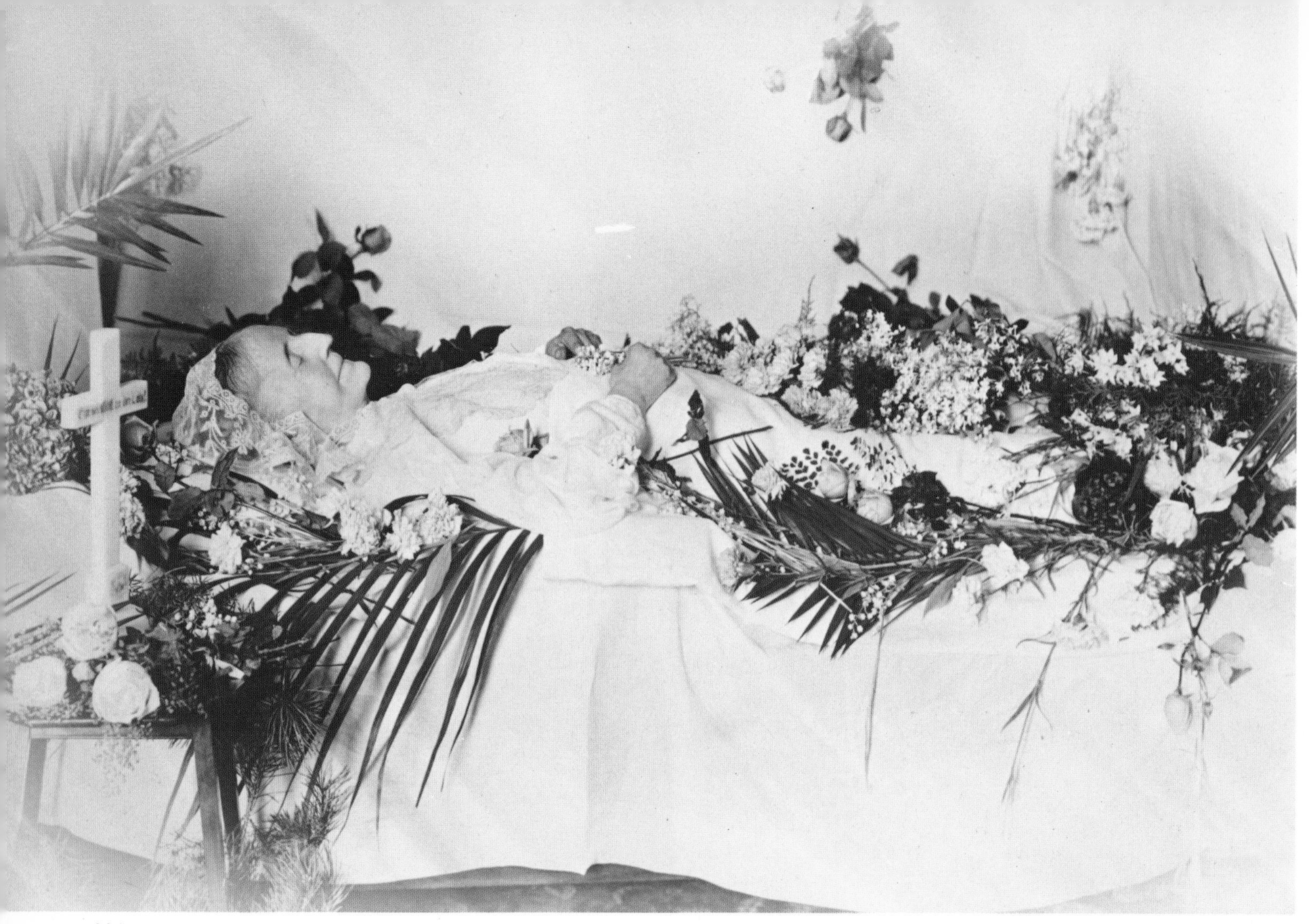

224

224 Queen Sophia of Sweden, wife of King Oscar II, on her deathbed, January 1914.

225 Prince Carl, second son of the Danish King Frederik VII, and Princess Maud of Denmark at home in Copenhagen with their son Prince Alexander, at the time of Carl's election as King of Norway, 1905. He was chosen by the Norwegian people, following the partition of the Kingdoms of Norway and Sweden, and mounted the Norwegian throne as King Haakon VII. His wife was the daughter of King Edward VII.

226 *Overleaf* Queen Louise of Denmark, wife of King Christian IX (second from right), and her daughters, Princess Alexandra (later Queen of Edward VII), Princess Dagmar (later Empress Marie of Russia) and Princess Thyra (later Duchess of Cumberland).

225

227 King Haakon and Queen Maud of Norway in coronation robes, 22 June 1906. Their coronation in Trondheim Cathedral was the last to take place in Scandinavia, and the second last on the European mainland (that of King Ferdinand and Queen Marie of Roumania at Alba Julia in 1922 was the last).

228 King Haakon VII of Norway swearing loyalty to the Norwegian constitution, Oslo, 27 November 1905.

229 King Christian IX and Queen Louise of Denmark with their family at Fredensborg Castle, 1895. Seated round the table, from left to right, are Prince Andrew of Greece (their grandson and father of Prince Philip, the present Duke of Edinburgh), his brother Prince Christopher of Greece; Grand Duchess Olga Alexandrovna of Russia (daughter of Empress Marie), Prince Hans of Schleswig-Holstein-Sonderburg-Glücksburg (brother of King Christian), Queen Olga of Greece, the Princess of Wales (later Queen Alexandra), King George I of Greece (son of King Christian), Queen Louise of Denmark, King Christian IX of Denmark, Dowager Empress Marie Feodorovna of Russia, Prince George of Greece (second son of George I), Princess Maud of Wales (later Queen Maud of Norway), Princess Marie of Greece (wife of Prince George), Princess Victoria of Wales and Grand Duke Michael Alexandrovich of Russia.

227

230 King Chulalongkorn of Siam, Prince George of Greece, Prince Waldemar of Denmark and Princess Marie of Denmark at Fredensborg Castle, 1897. King Chulalongkorn, on his two visits to Europe, forged links of friendship between the Siamese Royal Family and various European Royal Families which exist to the present day.

228

229

230

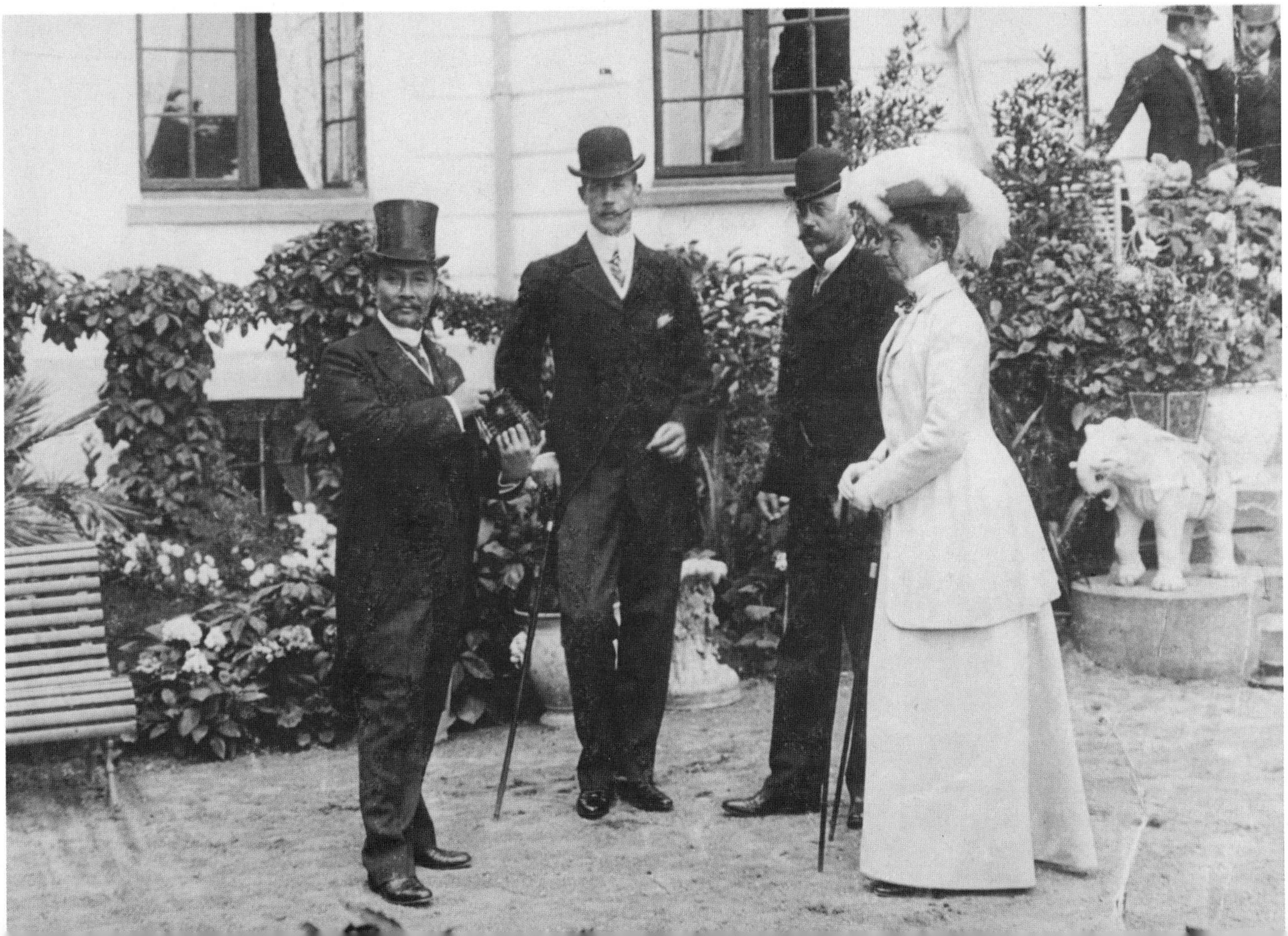

2

231 King Frederik VIII of Denmark playing cards with his sisters, left to right: Queen Alexandra, Dowager Empress Marie Feodorovna of Russia, the Duchess of Cumberland.

232 King Frederik VIII of Denmark and members of the Danish Royal Family on the beach.

233 A Royal cycling group at Fredensborg Castle, Denmark—from left to right, Prince Christian of Denmark (later King Christian X), Princess Marie-Louise of Baden, Princess Olga of Hanover, Grand Duchess Alexandra of Mecklenburg-Schwerin, Grand Duke Friedrich Franz IV of Mecklenburg-Schwerin, Prince Gustaf Adolf of Sweden (later King Gustaf VI Adolf). Last figure unknown.

234 King Frederik VIII of Denmark being greeted by schoolchildren on a visit to the provinces.

233

234

235 King Frederik VIII of Denmark, son of Christian IX, on the balcony of the Amalienborg Palace, Copenhagen, following his proclamation as King, January 1906.

236 Queen Louise of Denmark, wife of King Frederik VIII. She was known in family circles as the Swan, and this characteristic picture of her shows why.

235

236

237

238

237 Princess Margrethe of Denmark on the day of her confirmation. Although the Danish Royal Family is Lutheran it was decided at the time of the marriage of Prince Waldemar (son of King Christian IX) to Princess Marie of Orléans that any daughters of the marriage would be brought up in the Catholic faith. Princess Margrethe was their only daughter, and while her four brothers were brought up as Lutherans she followed her parents' decision. She later married Prince René of Bourbon-Parma.

238 Prince Harald, younger son of Frederik VIII, and his wife Princess Helena.

239 King Christian X, who succeeded to the throne in 1912, at a cabinet meeting in the Amalienborg Palace, Copenhagen (he is at the head of the table).

239

240

Iberia

The court of Spain is very ancient: its history can be traced back to late antiquity, when the Visigoths overran the Iberian peninsula. During the sixteenth and seventeenth centuries Spain was ruled by the Habsburgs, who after the Emperor Charles V (r. 1516–56) split into two lines, one holding court in Vienna and the other in Madrid. Under Charles and his son, Philip II, Spain achieved its golden age, an era as brilliant in its artistic and intellectual life as in its material prosperity. However, long religious struggles—against the Islamic occupier and the Jewish minority and finally against Christian heresy—made the court rather austere in both manners and morals.

Dynastic difficulties developed when Charles II (r. 1675–1700) failed to produce an heir, thereby prompting both Louis XIV of France and the Austrian Habsburgs to press their claims to the succession. A war lasting thirteen years (1701–14) concluded with the Bourbons in control of the Spanish throne. Troubles revived after Napoleon made his brother Joseph King of Spain (r. 1808–14), until the Duke of Wellington expelled the usurper and restored King Ferdinand VII. Ferdinand then altered the law of succession in favour of his three-year-old daughter, Isabella II, and to the detriment of his brother, Don Carlos. This brought about the enduring challenge of the Carlist faction, which broke out in bitter war during the new Queen's minority and the regency of her mother, Queen Cristina. By 1868 general turbulence resulted in Isabella's abdication and the establishment of a constitutional monarchy under Amadeus, Duke of Aosta—but only after the candidacy of a Hohenzollern triggered the Franco-Prussian War of 1870. Further disorders, including a new Carlist war, now forced the abdication of Amadeus, after only two years on the throne, and his replacement by first a republic and then Alfonso XII, Isabella II's son, then only seventeen. At his premature death in 1885, this monarch left two daughters and a pregnant wife, who six months later gave birth to Alfonso XIII, the only man in history to have been born King. Queen Maria Cristina acted as regent until her son came of age. In 1906 Alfonso XIII married Princess Victoria Eugenie of Battenberg, the only daughter of Queen Victoria's youngest child, Princess Beatrice. Despite continuous strife, Alfonso managed to reign until 1931, even to maintain the strict formality that was always characteristic of the Spanish court. In the same year, however, the monarchy was overthrown and a republic proclaimed, creating a volatile situation that exploded in the Spanish Civil War (1936–9). Hostilities ceased only with the dictatorship of General Francisco Franco. In 1947 the Generalissimo declared Spain a monarchy once more and thus set the stage for an eventual restoration. Juan Carlos, Alfonso's grandson, and his wife Sophie of Greece became King and Queen in 1975, and have succeeded in establishing a democracy despite right-wing attempts to reinstate a military dictatorship.

240 Queen Amalia of Portugal in riding habit on a fully-harnessed bull.

241 Queen Amalia of Portugal, wife of King Carlos I, receiving a *baise-main* from King Alfonso XIII of Spain, 1906.

Portugal's history was from early times intricately involved with that of Spain. In 1640 the country emerged from Spanish domination when John IV established the Braganza dynasty, which forged another link in the long alliance with England by providing a queen, Catherine, for King Charles II. With the Napoleonic invasion which came in

1807 the Portuguese royal family fled to Brazil, whence John VI did not return until 1821. The following year his son, Dom Miguel, became the Emperor of a Brazil that had now declared its independence. When Pedro, King John's successor, abdicated in 1826, it was his daughter, Maria II da Gloria, who in 1826 ascended the throne of Portugal. Although marred by challenge from Dom Miguel, involving coups and dictatorships, her reign saw a steady progress towards liberalization. In 1836 the Queen married Prince Ferdinand of Saxe-Coburg-Gotha, a first cousin of Queen Victoria's Albert. Unlike his English counterpart, Ferdinand was created King Consort, and after the death of his wife he became Regent for their son, Pedro V. In 1889 Carlos I, Pedro's nephew, succeeded to the throne; he married the Bourbon Princess Amélie d'Orléans, the daughter of the Comte de Paris, Pretender to the throne of France. To suppress the republican sentiments then growing in Portugal, King Carlos attempted to restore the authoritarian rule of old. This merely inspired his own assassination and that of his heir in 1908. Carlos's younger son succeeded as Manoel II, but revolution ended his brief reign after only two years. Thus, just as Portugal had anticipated the rest of Europe in the heroic age of its overseas expansion, it also anticipated in the modern era the events that would sweep away most of the courts of Europe.

242 The lying-in-state of King Carlos I and Crown Prince Luis of Portugal in the Saõ Vicente Church, Lisbon. Father and son were assassinated in Lisbon on 1 February 1908.

243 King Manoel II with his mother, the widowed Queen Amalia, on the terrace of the Castle de la Pena, Cintra, 1909.

244 King Manoel II (centre) at an open-air military mass in Lisbon, 1909.

245 *Overleaf* King Manoel II of Portugal, who succeeded to the throne on the assassinations of his father and his elder brother, reading the speech from the throne in the Cortes, April 1908. To his right is his uncle, the Infante Alfonso. Manoel's reign lasted a mere two years before he was deposed.

242

246

247

246 The wedding of King Manoel II and Queen Augusta Viktoria, 1913. From left to right, the Prince of Wales (later Duke of Windsor), Dowager Grand Duchess Luise of Baden, Princess Alexandra Viktoria of Prussia (behind), Queen Amalia of Portugal, Princess Elena of Savoy Duchess of Aosta (behind), King Manoel, Prince August Wilhelm of Prussia, Queen Augusta Viktoria, Prince Johann Georg of Saxony, next but one, Infante Carlos of Spain Prince of Bourbon-Two Sicilies, Prince Wilhelm of Hohenzollern and Prince Friedrich Viktor of Hohenzollern.

247 King Manoel being offered a light by M. Briand, president of the Council, while on a shoot at Rambouillet in France, 1909.

248 The exiled King Manoel II and Princess Augusta Viktoria of Hohenzollern on their wedding day—Sigmaringen, 4 September 1913.

249 Infante Miguel of Portugal, Duke of Braganza, and his second wife, Infanta Maria Teresa. Infante Miguel spent much of his life in exile—his father, King Miguel I, was deposed in 1834, and the latter's niece, Queen Maria II da Gloria, was placed on the throne. On the death of the last King of Portugal, the exiled Manoel II, in 1932, Infante Miguel's son, the Infante Duarte, the only surviving male member of the family, became head of the exiled Royal House of Portugal.

250 Portugal and Britain have had an unbroken treaty of friendship for some six hundred years. During his state visit to Britain in 1909 King Manoel took the opportunity to go hunting with King Edward VII in Windsor Great Park. He also had a tour of Eton.

248

249

250

251 Queen Maria Cristina of Spain with her daughter-in-law, Queen Victoria Eugenia. Born in 1887, 'Ena' was the daughter of Prince and Princess Henry of Battenberg and granddaughter of Queen Victoria.

252 King Alfonso XIII at the wheel of a Hispano-Suiza, 1913.

251

252

45089

253 King Alfonso XIII (seated on bridge, looking at camera) during military manoeuvres, 1909.

254 Queen Amalia of Portugal (left) and Queen Maria Cristina of Spain (centre) in the royal box at a bullfight in Madrid, 1906.

253

254

255 The Spanish Royal Family in about 1908. Seated, from left to right, Queen Maria Cristina, Infanta Maria de la Paz, Queen Victoria Eugenia and Infanta Isabel; standing, Infanta Luisa, King Alfonso XIII, Princess Maria del Pilar of Bavaria, Prince Ferdinand of Bavaria, Infante Carlos of Spain Prince of Bourbon-Two Sicilies, Prince Adalbert of Bavaria and Prince Ranieri of Bourbon-Two Sicilies.

255

256 The trousseau of Infanta Maria Teresa of Spain, on display in one of the rooms of the Oriente Palace, Madrid, 1906.

257 The wedding of Infanta Maria Teresa of Spain, sister of King Alfonso XIII, and Prince Ferdinand of Bavaria, 12 January 1906, in Madrid. Seated, left to right, Princess Louise of Bavaria, Queen Maria Cristina of Spain with Infanta Isabel Alfonsa of Spain Princess of Bourbon-Two Sicilies and Infante Alfonso of Spain Prince of Bourbon-Two Sicilies, and Princess Maria de la Paz of Bavaria. Standing, left to right, Princess Maria del Pilar of Bavaria, Infante Carlos of Spain Prince of Bourbon-Two Sicilies, Prince Georg of Bavaria, Infante Luis Fernando of Spain Prince of Orléans, Infanta Isabel of Spain, Prince Heinrich of Bavaria, Infanta Eulalia of Spain Princess of Orléans, Infante Alfonso of Spain Prince of Orléans, King Alfonso XIII, Prince Adalbert of Bavaria, Infanta Maria Teresa of Spain, Prince Ludwig Ferdinand of Bavaria, Prince Filippo of Bourbon-Two Sicilies, Prince Ferdinand of Bavaria, Prince Ranieri of Bourbon-Two Sicilies, Prince Konrad of Bavaria, Archduke Friedrich of Austria, Prince Gennaro of Bourbon-Two Sicilies and Prince Alfons of Bavaria.

257

258 Infanta Maria Cristina of Spain, younger daughter of King Alfonso, with her nurse.

259 King Alfonso XIII with one of his children.

260 King Alfonso (foreground, left) and Queen Victoria Eugenia (on the dais, centre) with the Cardinal of Burgos during the reburial of the remains of Spain's eleventh-century hero, El Cid.

259

260

261 The royal bathing-machine at San Sebastian.

262 King Alfonso's children, Infante Alfonso, Prince of the Asturias (1907–1938) and Infante Jaime (1908–1975), on the beach at San Sebastian.

262

261

263 From left to right, Princess Henry of Battenberg (youngest daughter of Queen Victoria and mother of Queen Victoria Eugenia of Spain), unknown figure, Infanta Isabel, Infante Jaime, Queen Victoria Eugenia, Queen Maria Cristina and Infante Alfonso, Prince of the Asturias, at a Scout Festival in Madrid.

263

264

265

Italy

264 King Vittorio Emanuele II of Italy. Formerly King of Sardinia, Vittorio Emanuele became the first King of united Italy in 1861.

265 King Umberto I, son of Vittorio Emanuele II (back to camera, leaning on sword), with a group of officers at Capanella.

Like Germany, Italy had existed from late antiquity onward as an agglomeration of disparate states and did not achieve full nationhood until the second half of the nineteenth century. But the whole spirit of *Risorgimento*, as the Italians called their drive towards national unification, became identified with the house of Savoy, which produced the monarch under whom the first pan-Italian government would be established. By 1870, Austria had been expelled from Lombardy and Venice in the north, the Bourbons from Naples and Sicily in the south, and the Pope from his political control of Rome and the Papal States, a power that had dominated since the

266 Queen Margherita of Italy, wife of King Umberto I.

267 King Vittorio Emanuele III and Queen Elena of Italy in one of the first cars, 1900. Queen Elena was the daughter of King Nicholas I of Montenegro.

266

267

268 King Vittorio Emanuele III and Emperor Wilhelm II in the Royal Gondola, Venice, 1908.

269

269 King Vittorio Emanuele III of Italy, son of King Umberto I, in fancy dress, 1902.

270 Princess Elena (Hélène) of Savoy, Duchess of Aosta (1871–1951) in court dress. Before her marriage to the Duke (King Vittorio Emanuele III's first cousin) she had hoped to marry Prince Albert, Duke of Clarence, the elder son of King Edward VII. Although both Queen Victoria and the Prince's parents were in favour of the marriage, the Pope was not prepared to allow Hélène, daughter of the Count of Paris, to change her religion, and so the marriage never took place. Prince Albert later became engaged to Princess Mary of Teck, who after the Prince's sudden death married his younger brother the Duke of York (the future King George V). It is interesting to speculate that had the Pope's decision been different it might have been the Duchess of Aosta, and not Queen Mary, who was crowned Queen of England in 1911.

fourth century. As Vittorio Emanuele II, the new nation's first King, said: 'Italy is like an artichoke which has to be eaten leaf by leaf,' and indeed the Italian monarchy came into existence only gradually as, one by one, the peninsula's various polities could be absorbed, through the efforts of Garibaldi, Cavour, and the monarch himself, into one coherent system. When this occurred, the Savoy dynasty established itself in Rome, there taking up residence in the Pope's old Quirinale Palace.

At first this new court was boycotted by the *Neri*, or 'Blacks', as the ancient Roman nobility called themselves. And it sparkled even less by reason of there being no consort. But the accession of Umberto I in 1878 gave Italy its first Queen. Herself a Savoy by birth, Queen Margherita was not only regal, but she also had a great love of music and the arts in general.

Umberto's assassination in 1900 brought his only son, Vittorio Emanuele III, to the throne. Despite his small stature, the new King had married a very tall and statuesque Princess, Elena of Montenegro, creating a disparity that photography seems to have made all the more pronounced. After a childhood and adolescence spent at the Russian court, Queen Elena had little difficulty in playing her role with dignity. The royal couple were devoted to one another and became the proud parents of one son, who, after his father's abdication, would be King Umberto II for one month in 1946, and four daughters who all inherited the dark good looks of the Montenegrin royal family.

271 The children of King Vittorio Emanuele III of Italy in the grounds of San Rossore, the royal residence near the sea between Pisa and Leghorn, 1911. From left to right, Princess Giovanna (later Queen of Bulgaria), Princess Yolanda, Princess Mafalda and Crown Prince Umberto (later King Umberto II).

272 Princess Elena of Savoy, Duchess of Aosta, serving soup to victims of the Naples earthquake, 1909.

273 *Overleaf* Princess Elena of Savoy, Duchess of Aosta on a visit to Africa, 1910.

271

272

70

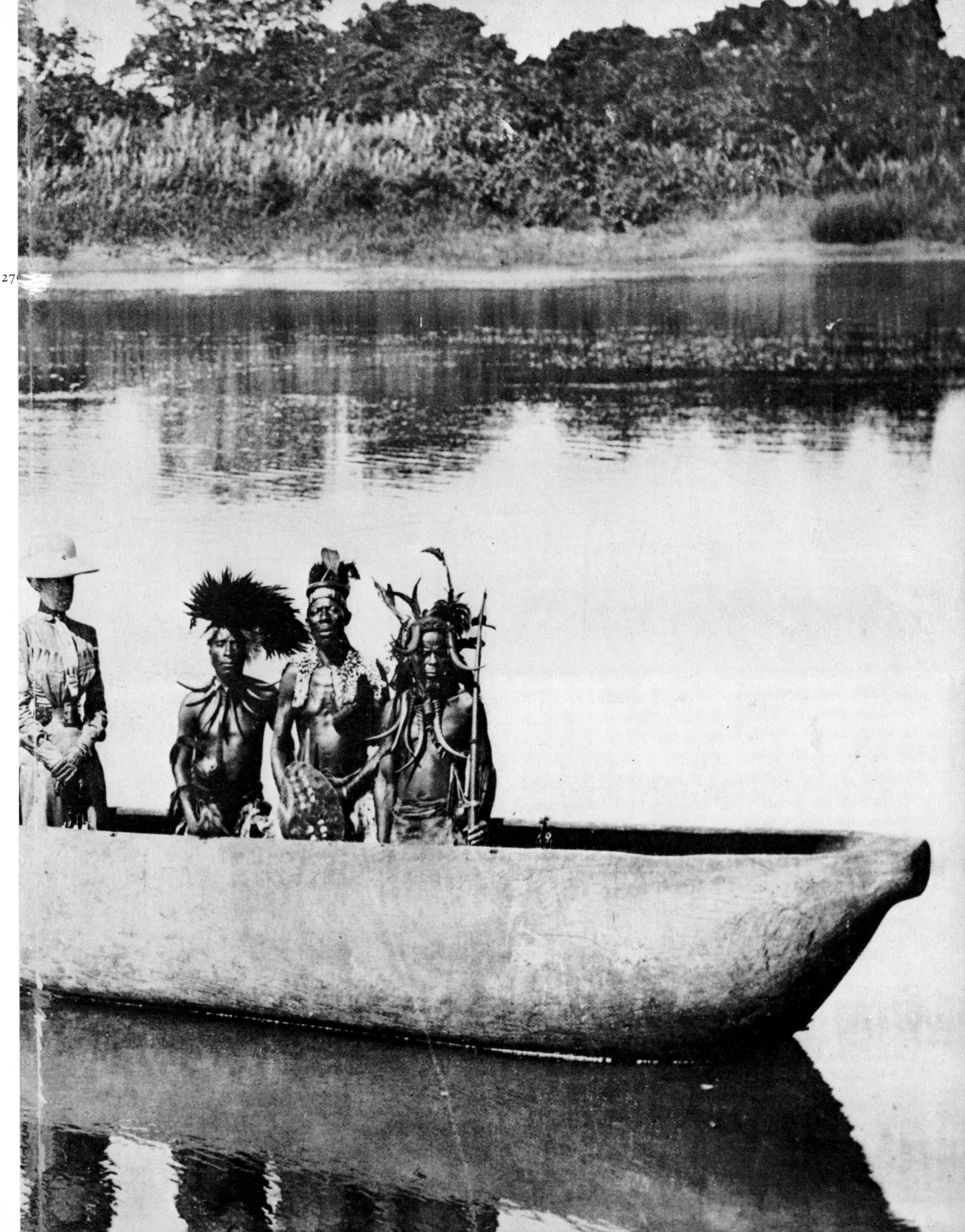

all manner of writers, artists, and musicians, and even played in her own orchestra at the palace in Bucharest. But perhaps more than anything else, Elisabeth loved to stand on the terrace of her house in Constanza watching the sea and occasionally shouting her blessings through a megaphone to departing ships. The beautiful Queen Marie, Elisabeth's successor, was the daughter of Prince Alfred, Duke of Edinburgh, the second son of Queen Victoria and Prince Albert. Queen Marie loved to dress in romantic clothes and great quantities of jewellery, and was often photographed among leopard-skins and arum lilies. The Roumanian dynasty survived until 1947.

After many centuries fiercely maintaining its independence of Turkey, Montenegro, the tiny state at the southern end of the Dinaric Alps, had its sovereignty formally recognized in 1860 under King Nicholas I, who reigned until 1918, when his country was absorbed into Serbia. So strategic was the location of Montenegro that at the capital, Cetinje, a small mountain town, virtually every other building housed a foreign legation. This enabled King Nicholas to marry off his daughters in a series of brilliant diplomatic alliances, which made him father-in-law to two Russian Grand Dukes as well as to the Kings of Serbia and Italy.

The last state to acquire a royal ruler was Albania. This occurred as late as 1914, only a few months before the outbreak of World War I, when Prince Wilhelm of Wied arrived in Tirana to found a dynasty. But shortly after the beginning of hostilities in

279

7

8

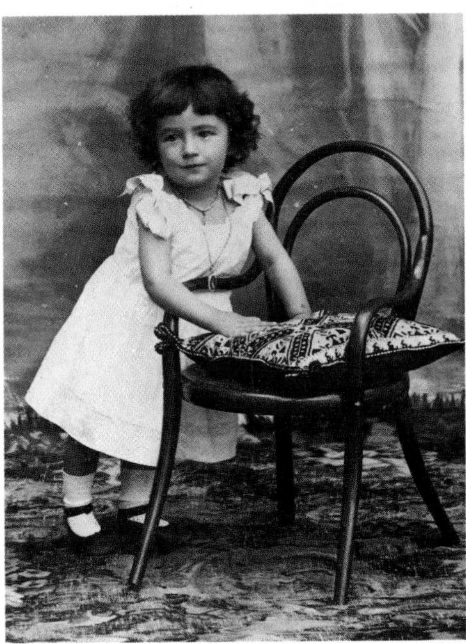

280

281

277 King Peter I of Serbia on the grand staircase of the Royal Palace, Belgrade, 1911.

278 King Ferdinand I of Bulgaria with his mother, Princess Clémentine, in the courtyard of the monastery at Tirnovo. Clémentine of Orléans was the youngest daughter of King Louis-Philippe of the French.

279 King Ferdinand I of Bulgaria (second from left) and Queen Eleonore (foreground), with Princess Eudoxie and Princess Nadejda (behind her), and Crown Prince Boris and Prince Kyril at a mass to commemorate King Ferdinand's accession—Tirnovo, 1912. The King's first wife, Princess Marie-Louise of Bourbon-Parma, had died in 1899. Both Ferdinand and Eleonore (formerly Princess Eleonore Reuss of the Younger Line) were 47 at the time of their marriage.

280 Crown Prince Boris of Bulgaria (the future King Boris III), the elder son of King Ferdinand I. It was the custom in many Royal families for young boys to be dressed as girls until the age of about four.

281 King Otto I of Greece in national costume. The second son of King Ludwig I of Bavaria, he was elected King of Greece in 1832 and reigned for thirty years until his deposition during the insurrection of 1862. The Greek throne was then offered to a number of European princes, including Prince Alfred, Duke of Edinburgh, second son of Queen Victoria. It was finally accepted by Prince Wilhelm of Denmark, second son of King Christian IX, who mounted the Greek throne as King George I.

282

August, Wilhelm repacked his bags and set sail for Germany, leaving the Albanian throne empty until President Ahmed Bey Zogu set himself upon it in 1928 as King Zog I. Eleven years later, in 1939, he was deposed by Mussolini.

Whatever the new Balkan courts may have lacked in splendour, relative to the more established courts in Central and Western Europe, they made up for in the flamboyant personalities who filled them. The new monarchies acquired something of a comic-opera reputation (Ruritania is always thought of as an imaginary Balkan state), and indeed the plot of Franz Lehár's *The Merry Widow*, one of the most popular operettas of all time, concerns a rich widow whose romance with a foreigner would threaten the transfer of her money abroad and thus the bankruptcy of Pontevedro, an imaginary country modelled upon Montenegro.

While the fictitious Pontevedro continues to enchant audiences all over the world, the true Montenegro disappeared into greater Serbia after World War I. It took another war and a series of Communist coups to bring down the thrones of Roumania, Bulgaria, and Yugoslavia (the former Serbia). Then, with the abolition of the Greek monarchy in 1967, Balkan court life ceased to exist, and the dynasties that had so briefly taken root and flourished in the unlikely soil of south-eastern Europe were no more.

283

282 Queen Olga of Greece, wife of King George I. Formerly Grand Duchess Olga Constantinovna of Russia, she came to Greece in 1867 as a bride of sixteen, securing the affections of the people of Athens by wearing a dress of blue and white, the national colours.

283 Princesses Olga, Elisabeth and Marina of Greece, the daughters of Prince Nicholas and Princess Helen. Princess Marina later married George, fourth son of King George V, and became the Duchess of Kent and mother of the present Duke, Princess Alexandra and Prince Michael.

284 Princess Marie of Greece, formerly Princess Marie Bonaparte, the wife of Prince George of Greece, on a visit to the ruins at Nicopolis, 1913.

284

285 King George I of Greece on his deathbed. He was assassinated at Salonika on 18 March 1913 while taking an evening stroll.

286 King Constantine I of Greece, with Queen Sophie (the sister of the German Emperor), Crown Prince George (right) and Prince Alexander (left), swearing loyalty to the constitution in the Greek Parliament, on his accession as King, March 1913.

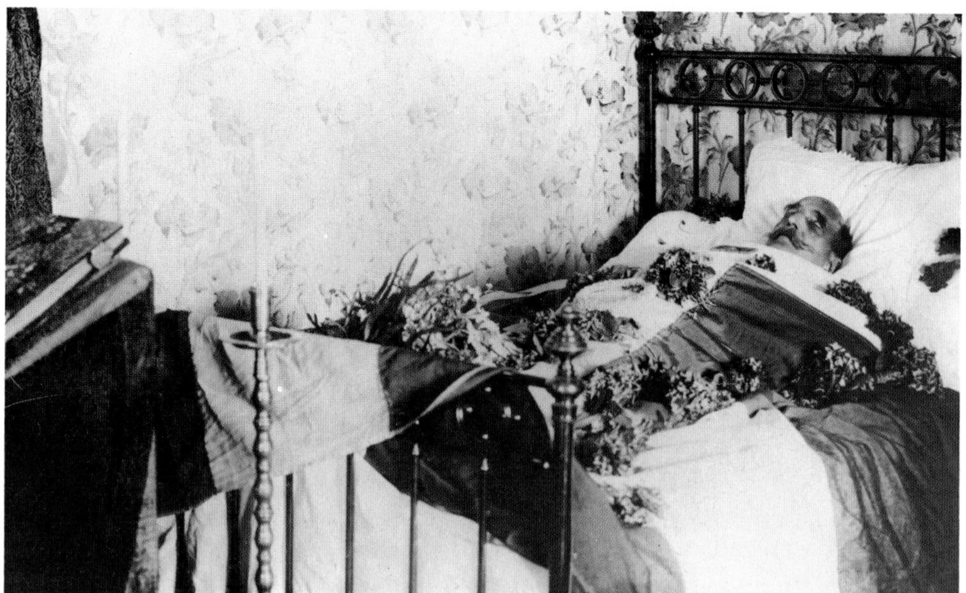

285

286

287 The Greek Royal Family at breakfast in the Royal Palace, Athens, 1913. Left to right, Princess Irene, Crown Prince George (later King George II), Queen Sophie with Princess Katherine, King Constantine, Princess Helen (later Queen of Roumania), Prince Alexander (later King Alexander I) and Prince Paul (later King Paul I).

289

290

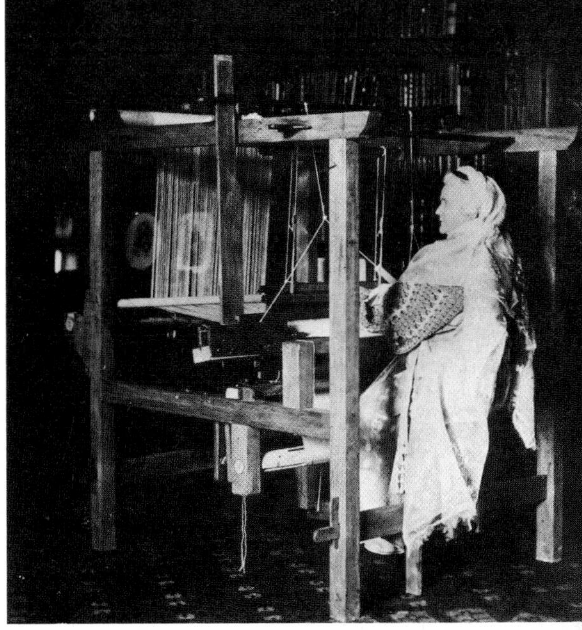

288 Prince Wilhelm I and Princess Sophie of Albania with their children, Hereditary Prince Carol Victor and Princess Marie Eleonore, walking through the streets of Durazzo, 1914. Prince Wilhelm, formerly Prince of Wied, was invited to become Prince of Albania in 1914; he arrived there in March of that year, but left six months later after the outbreak of World War I.

289 Queen Marie of Roumania delighted in exotic clothes and jewels. This photograph of her in her Byzantine boudoir at Castle Sinaia, seated on a leopard-skin and flanked by arum lilies, displays something of her theatricality, which gave the writer Elinor Glyn the inspiration for the central character of the Balkan queen in her novel *Three Weeks*.

290 Queen Elisabeth of Roumania at her loom.

288

291 The Russian Imperial Family photographed during their visit to Constanza in June 1914. It was hoped that Nicholas's eldest daughter, Olga, and King Carol's grandson, Carol, would become engaged at this time, but as neither was keen on the idea their families did not force them into it. From left to right, Grand Duchess Marie Nicolaievna, King Carol I, Grand Duchess Anastasia Nicolaievna, Princess Marie of Roumania, Empress Alexandra Feodorovna, Prince Carol of Roumania, Grand Duchess Olga Nicolaievna with Princess Ileana of Roumania, Crown Prince Ferdinand, Crown Princess Marie, Queen Elisabeth, Emperor Nicholas II, and Grand Duchess Tatiana Nicolaievna with Prince Mircea of Roumania. Seated in the foreground, the Tsarevich Alexis Nicolaievich and Prince Nicholas of Roumania. This was the last time the Russian Imperial couple were seen by foreign relations.

292 Queen Elisabeth of Roumania (1843–1916) performing with her orchestra at a concert she gave in 1902.

293 Princess Natalia of Montenegro on her wedding day, 25 July 1902.

294 Crown Prince Danilo of Montenegro. It was the Kingdom of Montenegro that inspired the Austrian composer Franz Lehár to write his most popular operetta, *The Merry Widow*. Crown Prince Danilo was later to bring a successful action against an American film company for Erich von Stroheim's portrayal of 'Prince Danilo' in a 1930s production of the operetta.

295 The delicate political situation in the Balkans during the reign of King Nicholas I of Montenegro enabled him to marry off his children in a series of brilliant matches—his eldest daughter, Princess Zorka, married the future King Peter I of Serbia; his second and third daughters, Princess Militza and Princess Stana, married Russian Grand Dukes; his fifth daughter, Princess Elena, became Queen of Italy, and his sixth daughter, Princess Anna, married Prince Franz Josef of Battenberg. King Nicholas is photographed here with his

entire family. Back row, from left to right, Grand Duke Peter Nicolaievitch of Russia, Prince Franz Josef of Battenberg, Princess Vera of Montenegro, Princess Xenia of Montenegro, Crown Prince Danilo of Montenegro, Prince Mirko of Montenegro and Prince Peter of Montenegro. Seated, left to right, Crown Princess Militza of Montenegro, Grand Duchess Militza Nicolaievna of Russia, Queen Elena of Italy, Queen Milena, King Nicholas, Princess Anna of Battenberg, King Vittorio Emanuele III of Italy and Princess Natalia of Montenegro. Seated in foreground, Princess Helen of Serbia, Grand Duchess Anastasia Nicolaievna of Russia and Crown Prince Alexander of Serbia. There is a slight mystery about this photograph: it is not explained why Princess Anna (seated third from right) is in full evening dress with a tiara and orders, while the other ladies are in day dresses with hats.

293

294

295

296

296 King Nicholas of Montenegro greeting his troops in the streets of his capital, Cetinje, in 1910.

297 King Nicholas on the balcony of the Royal Palace (a two-storeyed villa) after the Montenegrin victory when Scutari fell, April 1913. The King was acclaimed by the wounded and by the women and children of the town—the army was still in the field.

The Eleventh Hour

On 6 May 1910 King Edward VII died in Buckingham Palace, after a relatively short reign of nine years. A great gathering of Kings and Queens assembled in the capital for his funeral, among them the German Emperor, Wilhelm II. This was the first of many great royal gatherings taking place throughout Europe in the four years leading up to the First World War; these ceremonies were to prove the swansong of the old order of European royalty.

In June of the following year, 1911, King George V and Queen Mary were crowned in Westminster Abbey and the following month their eldest son, Prince Edward, was invested as Prince of Wales in Caernarvon Castle. Later the same year the King and Queen travelled to India for what was possibly the greatest of all Imperial ceremonies, the Coronation Durbar at Delhi, where they were installed as Emperor and Empress of India.

In October 1911 Archduke Karl of Austria was married to Princess Zita of Bourbon-Parma. The wedding was attended by the aged Emperor Franz Josef, whom Archduke Karl was to succeed five years later.

On the very eve of the First World War, in 1913, Russia and Germany both celebrated royal occasions. Throughout 1913 the Russian Empire staged a series of celebrations to mark the tercentenary of the Romanov Dynasty, with the entire family appearing in public to receive the acclaim of the Russian people. Five years later eighteen members of the Imperial Family were to lose their lives in the Bolshevik Revolution.

In May 1913 the German Emperor, Wilhelm II, invited King George V and Emperor Nicholas II of Russia to Berlin for the marriage of his daughter, Princess Viktoria Luise, to Prince Ernst August of Hanover. There was a rich irony in this, for a year later the two great rulers who danced with the Princess at her wedding ball were at war with her father.

In retrospect the years leading up to the war seem a galaxy of royal events. As its eleventh hour approached, the old order flashed and glittered as if determined to carry on for ever. How, one wonders, would life have been in the great courts of Europe if they had not been drawn into the conflict which was to end with the fall of the mightiest? Of those that remain most are little more than objects of curiosity, relics of a bygone age. The era of royal pomp and magnificence is virtually extinguished.

298 The Coronation Durbar at Delhi, December 1911. Although Queen Victoria had been proclaimed Empress of India in 1877 it was her grandson, King George V, who was the first and only British monarch to be installed as Emperor at Delhi. King George and Queen Mary travelled to India the year after their accession and on 12 December 1911 a vast open-air durbar (or court) was held, in the fashion of Indian royalty. Maharajahs and Nawabs travelled from all over the sub-continent to pay homage to their suzerain. In this photograph the Deb Rajah of Bhutan stands before the Imperial Dais. Flanking the throne are seven pages, all princes, drawn from the ranks of Indian royalty. To the left of the throne are the Viceroy and Vicereine of India.

299 King George and Queen Mary at the Coronation Durbar at Delhi, 12 December 1911. The King is wearing the Crown of India, specially made for the occasion as there were fears about taking the State Crown out of Britain.

300 The investiture of the Prince of Wales at Caernarvon Castle, 13 July 1911: Prince Edward kneels before his father King George V. Although the heir to the throne of England had borne the title Prince of Wales since the fourteenth century, this was the first time that an investiture ceremony had been held.

301 Throughout the summer of 1913 the tercentenary of the Romanov Dynasty was celebrated in Russia. In this photograph Emperor Nicholas II and the Tsarevich Alexis are seen leaving the Cathedral of Kazan.

302 At the investiture ceremony, the Prince of Wales walks between his parents.

301

302

303

303 King George V (right) and Emperor Nicholas II of Russia photographed together in Berlin, on the occasion of the marriage of Princess Viktoria Luise (only daughter of the Kaiser), in 1913. This wedding, just one year before the outbreak of the First World War, brought together the German Emperor and Empress, the British King and Queen and the Russian Emperor and Empress—they were never to meet again.

305

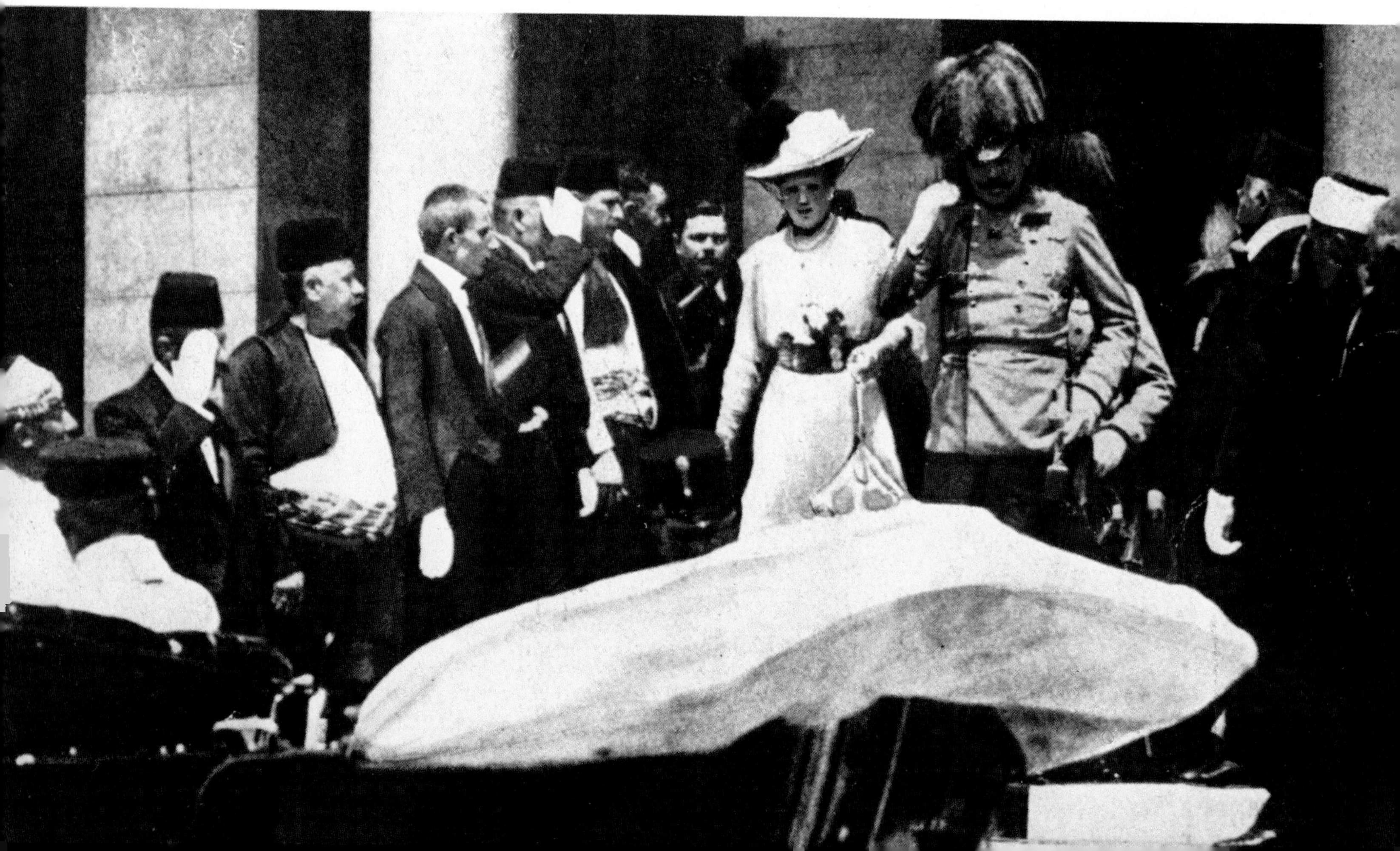

304 Crowds hailing Emperor Nicholas II, the Empress and the Tsarevich in the Kremlin, Moscow, during the tercentenary celebrations. They had just returned from a progress through the oldest towns in Russia, and the Emperor thanked the people for their expressions of loyalty on this journey: a speech perhaps remembered with bitterness five years later.

305 Archduke Franz Ferdinand of Austria and his wife, the Duchess of Hohenberg, at Sarajevo, moments before their assassination, 28 June 1914.

306 28 June 1914: a police arrest at Sarajevo, not of the assassin Gavrilo Princip, but probably of his accomplice Ferdinand Behr.

307 The funeral cortège of Archduke Franz Ferdinand and the Duchess of Hohenberg passing through the streets of Sarajevo, June 1914.

307

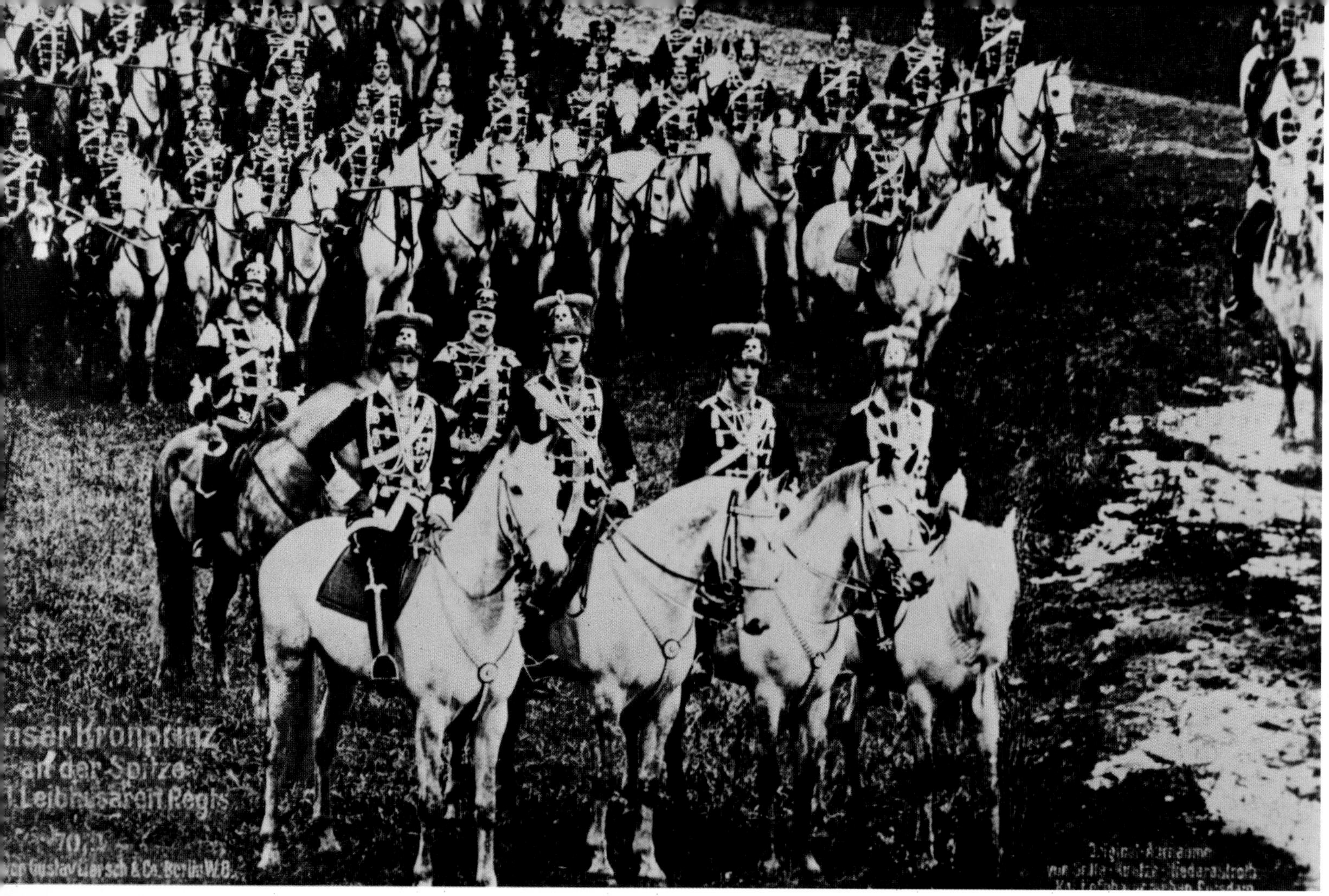

308

309

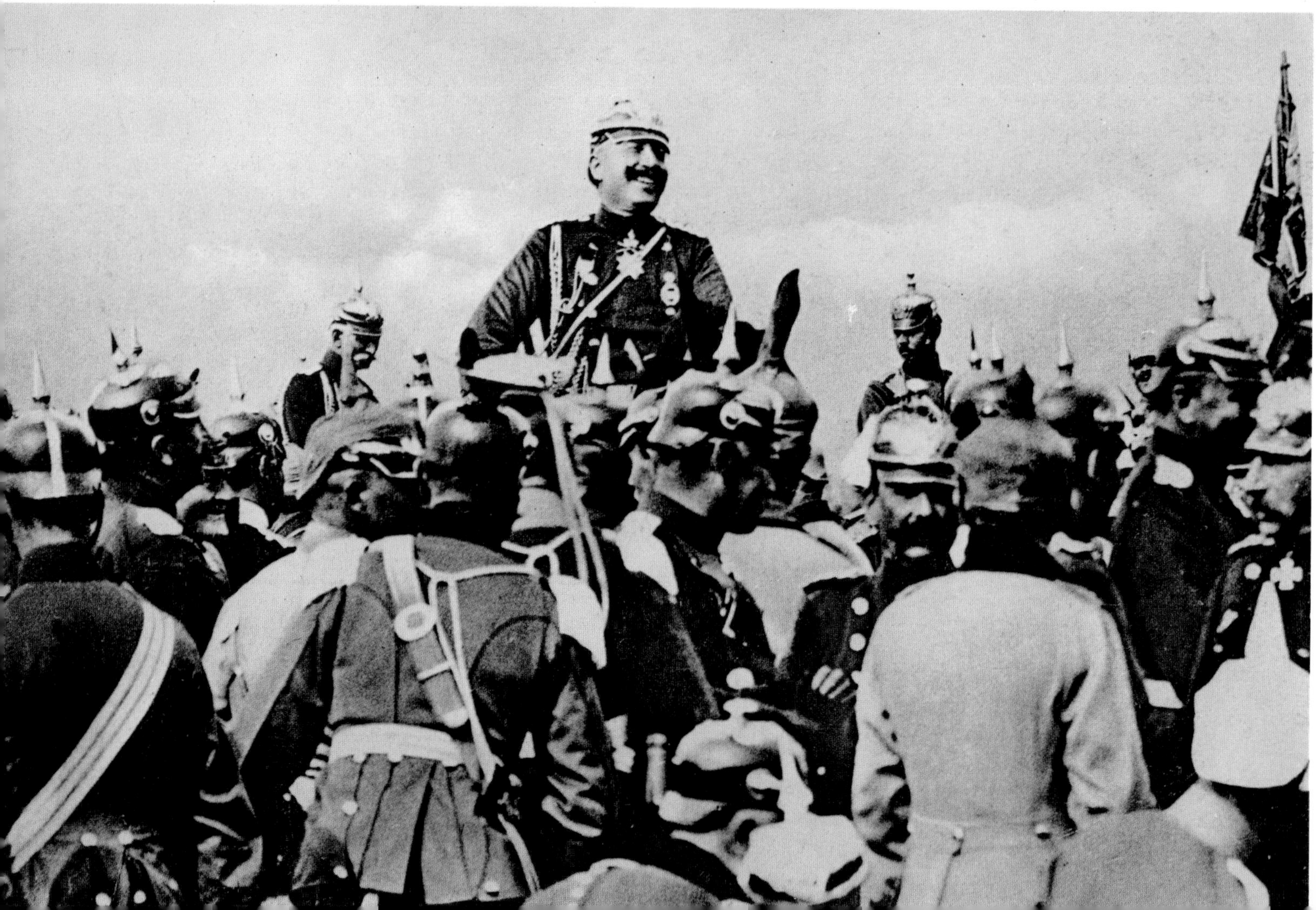

308 Crown Prince Wilhelm of Prussia with the Leibhusaren ('Death's Head') Regiment at Danzig.

309 Emperor Wilhelm II surrounded by a group of officers, 1912.

310 King George V working in the gardens of Buckingham Palace during the First World War, attended by Lord Stamfordham.

311 King Nicholas of Montenegro visiting the wounded at the Red Cross Hospital in Cetinje.

310

311

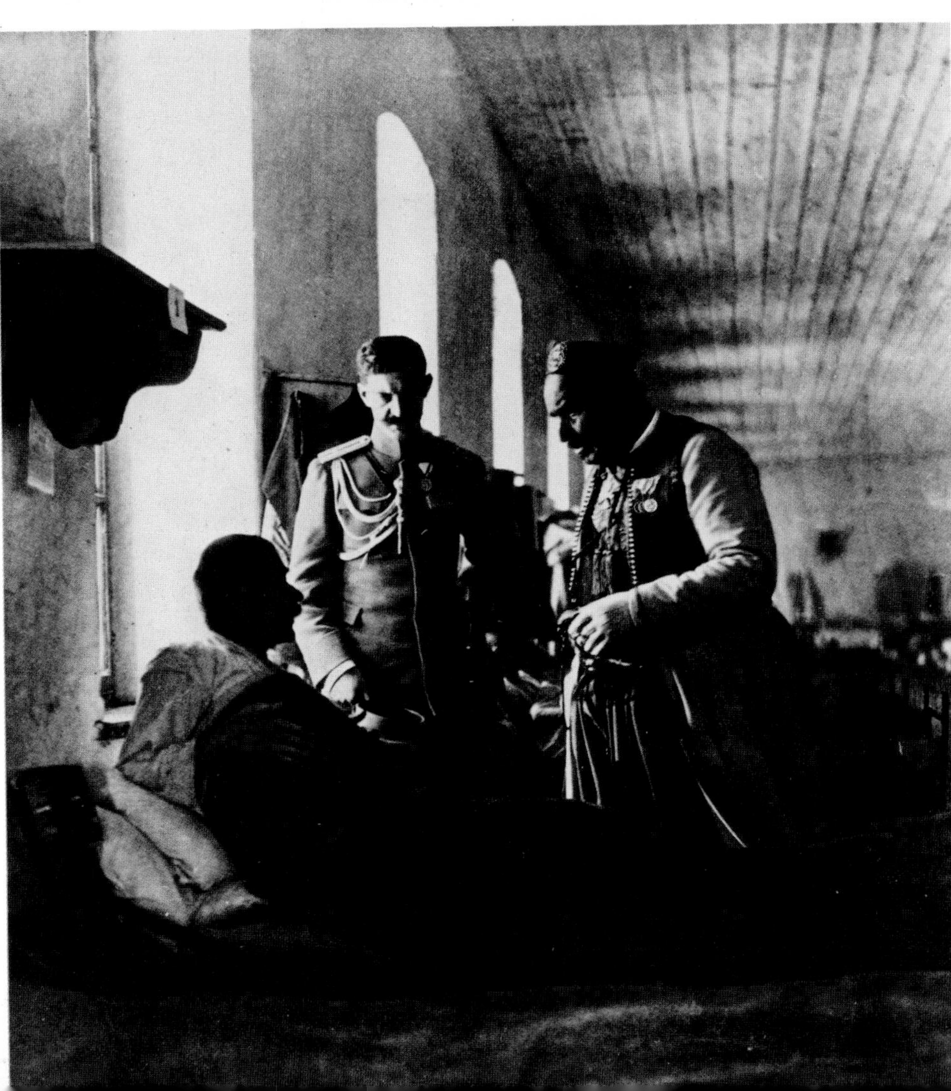

312 Queen Marie of Roumania nursing the wounded, 1916.

313 Empress Alexandra Feodorovna (to right) with her two eldest daughters, Olga and Tatiana, assisting at an operation in a Russian military hospital, January 1915.

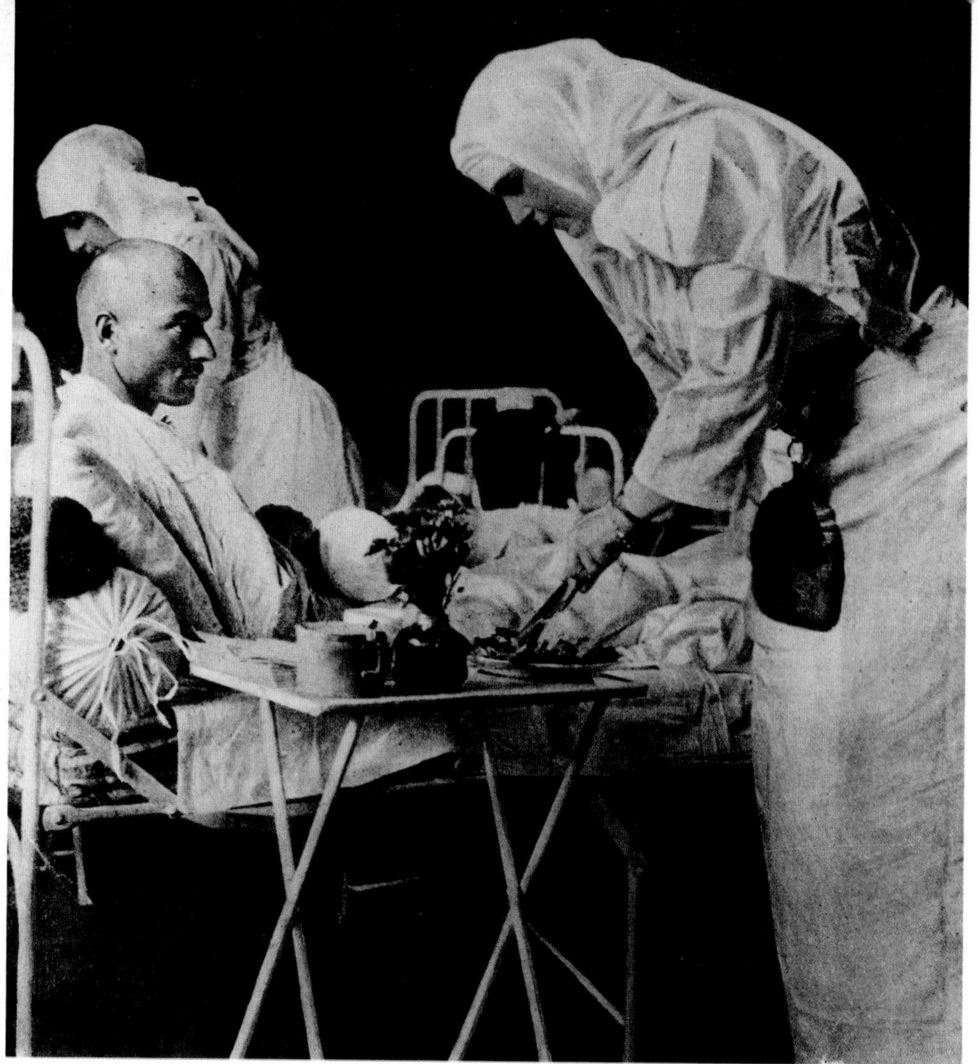

312

313

314

314 The lying-in-state of Emperor Franz Josef I of Austria in the Hofburg Chapel, Vienna, November 1916. Placed around the catafalque are the four crowns of the Austro-Hungarian Empire: the Imperial Crown of Austria, the Crown of St Stephen of Hungary, the Royal Crown of Bohemia and the Archducal Crown of Austria.

315 Emperor Karl I and Empress Zita of Austria with Crown Prince Otto on the day of their coronation as King and Queen of Hungary at Budapest, 20 December 1916.

315

Genealogical Table

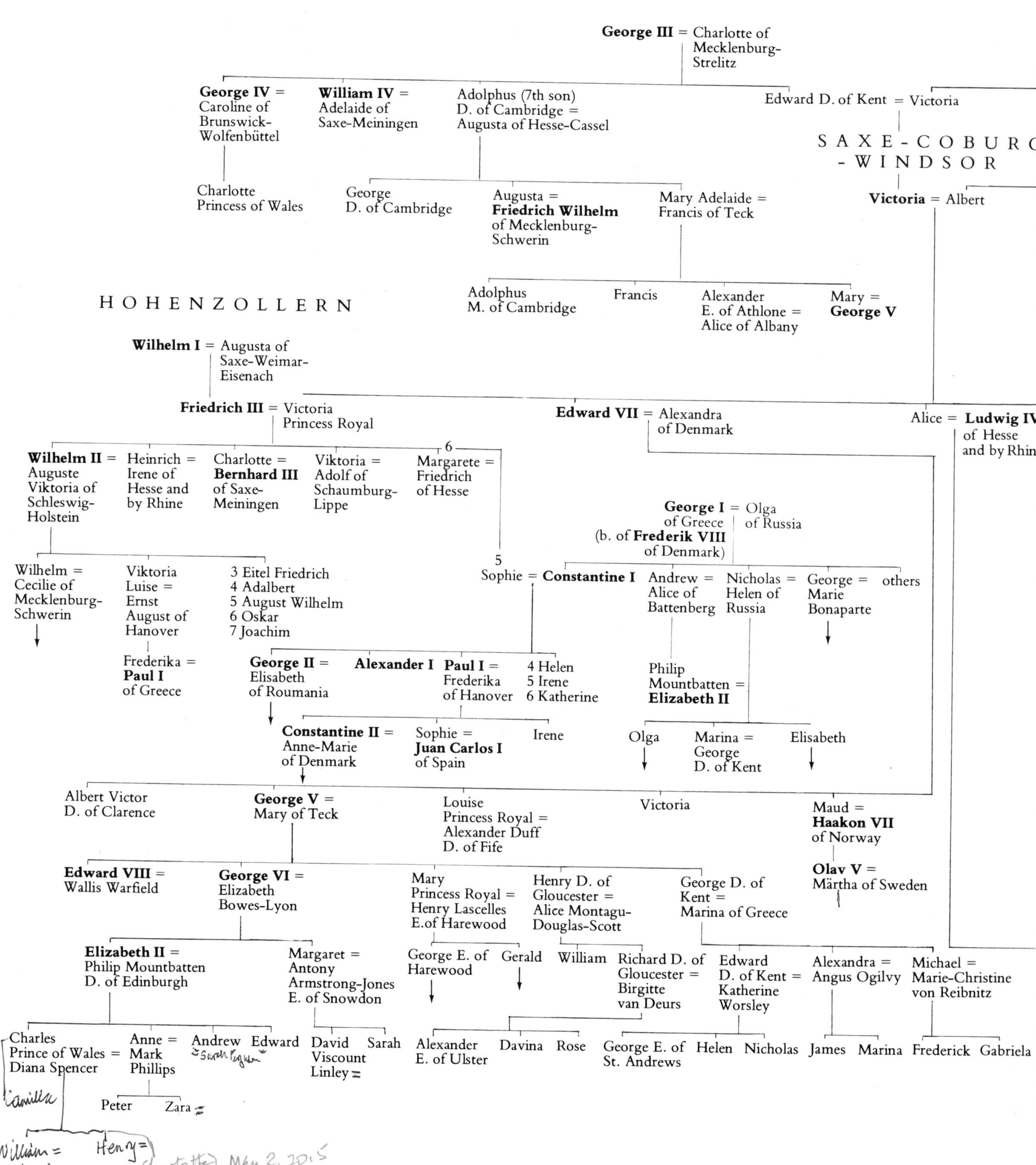

H A B S B U R G

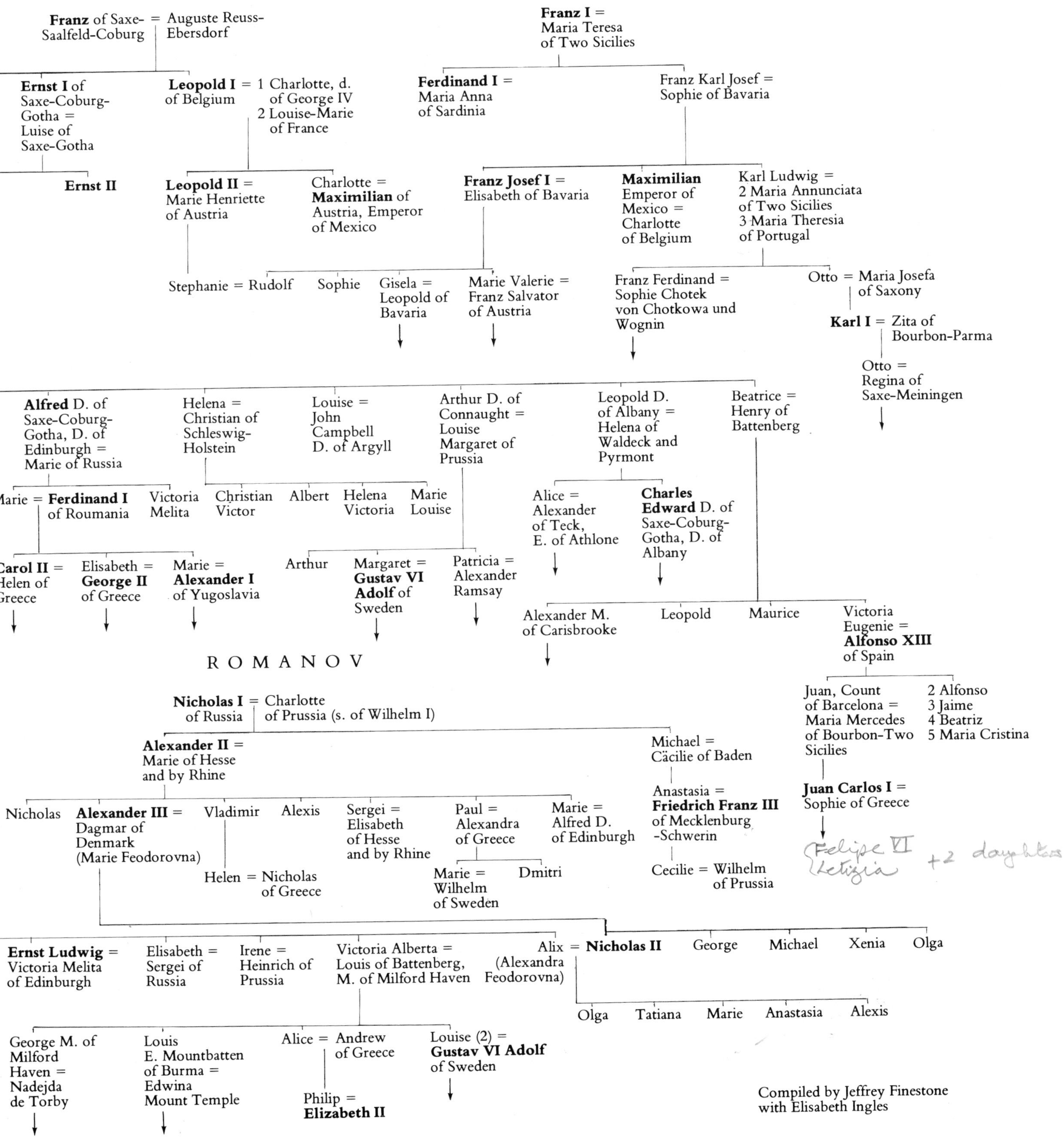

Franz of Saxe-Saalfeld-Coburg = Auguste Reuss-Ebersdorf
Ernst I of Saxe-Coburg-Gotha = Luise of Saxe-Gotha
Ernst II
Leopold I of Belgium = 1 Charlotte, d. of George IV 2 Louise-Marie of France
Leopold II = Marie Henriette of Austria
Charlotte = Maximilian of Austria, Emperor of Mexico
Franz I = Maria Teresa of Two Sicilies
Ferdinand I = Maria Anna of Sardinia
Franz Karl Josef = Sophie of Bavaria
Franz Josef I = Elisabeth of Bavaria
Maximilian Emperor of Mexico = Charlotte of Belgium
Karl Ludwig = 2 Maria Annunciata of Two Sicilies 3 Maria Theresia of Portugal
Stephanie = Rudolf
Sophie
Gisela = Leopold of Bavaria
Marie Valerie = Franz Salvator of Austria
Franz Ferdinand = Sophie Chotek von Chotkowa und Wognin
Otto = Maria Josefa of Saxony
Karl I = Zita of Bourbon-Parma
Otto = Regina of Saxe-Meiningen
Alfred D. of Saxe-Coburg-Gotha, D. of Edinburgh = Marie of Russia
Helena = Christian of Schleswig-Holstein
Louise = John Campbell D. of Argyll
Arthur D. of Connaught = Louise Margaret of Prussia
Leopold D. of Albany = Helena of Waldeck and Pyrmont
Beatrice = Henry of Battenberg
Marie = Ferdinand I of Roumania
Victoria Melita
Christian Victor
Albert
Helena Victoria
Marie Louise
Alice = Alexander of Teck, E. of Athlone
Charles Edward D. of Saxe-Coburg-Gotha, D. of Albany
Carol II = Helen of Greece
Elisabeth = George II of Greece
Marie = Alexander I of Yugoslavia
Arthur
Margaret = Gustav VI Adolf of Sweden
Patricia = Alexander Ramsay
Alexander M. of Carisbrooke
Leopold
Maurice
Victoria Eugenie = Alfonso XIII of Spain
Juan, Count of Barcelona = Maria Mercedes of Bourbon-Two Sicilies
2 Alfonso
3 Jaime
4 Beatriz
5 Maria Cristina
Juan Carlos I = Sophie of Greece
Felipe VI Letizia +2 daughters
R O M A N O V
Nicholas I of Russia = Charlotte of Prussia (s. of Wilhelm I)
Alexander II = Marie of Hesse and by Rhine
Michael = Cäcilie of Baden
Anastasia = Friedrich Franz III of Mecklenburg-Schwerin
Cecilie = Wilhelm of Prussia
Nicholas
Alexander III = Dagmar of Denmark (Marie Feodorovna)
Vladimir
Alexis
Sergei = Elisabeth of Hesse and by Rhine
Paul = Alexandra of Greece
Marie = Alfred D. of Edinburgh
Helen = Nicholas of Greece
Marie = Wilhelm of Sweden
Dmitri
Ernst Ludwig = Victoria Melita of Edinburgh
Elisabeth = Sergei of Russia
Irene = Heinrich of Prussia
Victoria Alberta = Louis of Battenberg, M. of Milford Haven
Alix (Alexandra Feodorovna) = Nicholas II
George
Michael
Xenia
Olga
Olga
Tatiana
Marie
Anastasia
Alexis
George M. of Milford Haven = Nadejda de Torby
Louis E. Mountbatten of Burma = Edwina Mount Temple
Alice = Andrew of Greece
Philip = Elizabeth II
Louise (2) = Gustav VI Adolf of Sweden
Compiled by Jeffrey Finestone with Elisabeth Ingles

Bibliography

SAXE-COBURG-WINDSOR

Elizabeth Longford, *Victoria R.I.* London: Weidenfeld and Nicolson, 1964.
Theodore Martin, *The Life of His Royal Highness the Prince Consort.* London: Smith, Elder, & Co., 1875–80.
Philip Magnus, *King Edward the Seventh.* London: John Murray, 1964.
Sidney Lee, *King Edward VII: A Biography.* London: Macmillan and Co., 1925–27.
Virginia Cowles, *Edward VII and His Circle.* London: Hamish Hamilton, 1958.
Georgina Battiscombe, *Queen Alexandra.* London: Constable & Co., 1969; Boston: Houghton Mifflin, 1969.
Harold Nicolson, *King George the Fifth: His Life and Reign.* London: Constable & Co., 1952.
James Pope-Hennessy, *Queen Mary, 1867–1953.* London: Allen & Unwin, 1959; New York: Knopf, 1959.
Frances Donaldson, *Edward VIII.* London: Weidenfeld and Nicolson, 1974; Philadelphia: Lippincott, 1975.
Frederick Ponsonby, *Recollections of Three Reigns.* London: Eyre and Spottiswoode, 1951.
James Laver, *Edwardian Promenade.* Boston: Houghton Mifflin, 1958.

HOHENZOLLERN

Virginia Cowles, *The Kaiser.* London: Collins, 1963.
Michael Balfour, *The Kaiser and His Times.* London: Cresset Press, 1964; Boston: Houghton Mifflin, 1964.
William II, *My Early Life.* New York: G. H. Doran Co., 1926.
Meriel Buchanan, *Victorian Gallery.* London: Cassell, 1956.
Walburga Paget, *Embassies of Other Days and Further Recollections.* London: Hutchinson & Co., 1923.

ROMANOV

Edward John Byng (ed.), *The Letters of Tsar Nicholas and Empress Marie, Being the Confidential Correspondence between Nicholas II, Last of the Tsars, and His Mother, Dowager Empress Maria Feodorovna.* London: Nicolson and Watson Ltd., 1937.
Sof'ya Karlovna Buxhoeveden, *The Life and Tragedy of Alexandra Feodorovna, Empress of Russia.* London: Longman, 1928.
Lili Dehn, *The Real Tsaritsa.* London: T. Butterworth Ltd., 1922.
Pierre Gilliard, *Thirteen Years at the Russian Court (A Personal Record of the Last Thirteen Years and Death of the Czar Nicholas II and His Family)*, trans. by F. Appleby Holt. London: Hutchinson & Co., 1921.
A. A. Mossolov, *At the Court of the Last Tsar.* London: Methuen, 1935.
Ian Vorres, *The Last Grand Duchess: Her Imperial Highness Grand Duchess Olga Alexandrovna.* London: Hutchinson, 1964.
Anna Aleksandrova Vyrubova, *Memories of the Russian Court.* New York: Macmillan, 1923.
Robert K. Massie, *Nicholas and Alexandra.* New York: Atheneum, 1967; London: Gollancz, 1967.

HABSBURG

Edward Crankshaw, *The Fall of the House of Hapsburg.* London: Longman, 1963.
Frederic Morton, *A Nervous Splendor: Vienna, 1888/1889.* Boston: Little, Brown, 1979; London: Weidenfeld and Nicolson, 1980.
Barbara Tuchman, *The Proud Tower: A Portrait of the World before the War, 1890–1914.* New York and London: Macmillan, 1966.
Gene Smith, *Maximilian and Carlota: A Tale of Romance and Tragedy.* New York: Morrow, 1973; London: Harrap, 1974.

Acknowledgements

The authors and John Calmann and Cooper Ltd. would like to express their thanks to the following for permission to reproduce the photographs in this book:
Bibliothèque Nationale, Paris: 85, 164, 199, 264, 266.
Bilderdienst Süddeutscher Verlag, Munich: 32, 56, 60, 75, 76, 146, 147, 148, 149, 150, 151, 154, 155, 156, 157.
Elsevier, Amsterdam: 191.
Hofburg Collection, Vienna: 88, 89, 90, 91, 94, 95, 97, 99, 100, 101, 102, 104, 107, 108, 109, 315.
Hoffotograf Elfelt, Copenhagen: 59, 226, 230, 231, 233, 236, 237, 238, 239, 282.
Illustrated London News: 61.
L'Illustration, Paris, and Editions Baschet: 43, 44, 62, 63, 66, 67, 72, 74, 84, 113, 128, 133, 136, 141, 142, 153, 169, 173, 175, 185, 186, 193, 203, 208, 209, 219, 241, 242, 243, 244, 245, 247, 250, 254, 256, 257, 268, 271, 272, 273, 277, 279, 284, 286, 287, 288, 291, 297, 301, 304, 311.
Mansell Collection, London: 119.
H.R.H. Prince Michael of Greece: 12, 21, 46, 86, 131, 132, 231, 270, 273, 287.
Nordiska Museet, Stockholm: 218, 220.
Popperfoto, London: 112, 137, 145, 298.
Radio Times Hulton Picture Library, London: 52, 92, 93, 305, 306.
Royal Archives, The Hague: 158, 183, 184, 187, 188, 190, 192.
Royal Collection, by gracious permission of Her Majesty the Queen: 11, 14, 15, 16, 18, 23, 25, 27, 28, 30, 31, 33, 36, 37, 38, 39, 40, 41, 50, 51, 68, 130, 134, 159, 165, 171, 227, 229, 240, 281, 310.
Royal Collection, Stockholm: 213, 214, 215, 216, 217, 221, 224.
Royal Library, Copenhagen: 232, 234, 235.
Snark International, Paris: 120, 121, 198, 265.
John Topham Picture Library, London: 34, 135.
Ullstein Bilderdienst, Berlin: 6, 69, 73, 96, 98, 103, 105, 114, 116, 117, 122, 123, 124, 125, 126, 127, 129, 132, 138, 139, 140, 144, 152, 160, 161, 163, 166, 168, 189, 197, 222, 223, 225, 248, 269, 275, 292, 296, 308, 314.
Roger Viollet, Paris: 1, 2, 4, 5, 7, 8, 9, 10, 19, 20, 26, 35, 42, 45, 48, 49, 57, 71, 87, 110, 115, 118, 170, 172, 174, 176, 177, 178, 181, 182, 194, 200, 201, 202, 204, 205, 206, 207, 210, 212, 228, 249, 251, 252, 253, 255, 258, 259, 260, 261, 262, 263, 274, 278, 280, 285, 290, 293, 295, 300, 302, 307, 309, 312, 313.
Yale University: 64, 65, 77, 78, 79, 80, 81, 82.
The other photographs are in private collections.

We should also like to thank John Murray (Publishers) Ltd. for permission to quote the excerpt from *King Edward the Seventh* by Sir Philip Magnus on page 13; Constable & Co. Ltd. for the excerpt from *Queen Alexandra* by Georgina Battiscombe on page 13; and Macmillan Ltd. and E. P. Dutton for the excerpt from *Recollections of Three Reigns* by Sir Frederick Ponsonby on page 16.

Index

Page numbers in *italic* refer to the illustrations